max science primary

DISCOVERING THROUGH ENQUIRY

Student Book 4

SUNETRA BERRY

SERIES EDITOR: **BOB KIBBLE**

macmillan education

INTERNATIONAL CURRICULUM

Macmillan Education
4 Crinan Street
London N1 9XW
A division of Springer Nature Limited

Companies and representatives throughout the world

Student Book ISBN 978-1-380-02163-2
Digital Student Pack ISBN 978-1-380-02426-8
Student Bundle Pack ISBN 978-1-380-02428-2

First published 2019

Original design by EMC Design Ltd and Macmillan Education
Page make-up by Ink Design
Illustrated by Natalie and Tamsin Hinrichsen, Sean Strydom, Marna Hattingh, Chris Venter, Bev Victor
Natalie and Tamsin Hinrichsen pp 7, 12, 24 (top & bottom), 15, 17, 20, 21, 22, 25 (bottom), 26, 29, 73, 74 (top), 76, 79, 80, 86, 92, 114, 115, 116, 117, 118, 119, 120, 121, 122, 124, 125, 128; Sean Strydom pp 13, 18, 19, 25 (top), 35, 36, 41 (top), 42, 44, 48, 55, 56, 57, 58, 62, 63 (top), 97, 98, 99, 100, 101, 102, 103, 104, 105, 106, 109, 111, 112; Marna Hattingh pp 34, 35, 39, 41 (bottom), 46, 47, 49, 50, 107, 110; Chris Venter pp 61, 63 (bottom), 65, 68, 70, 74 (bottom), 82; Bev Victor pp 45, 51, 95
Cover design by Sparks Publishing Services Ltd and Macmillan Education
Cover illustration by Star Publishing Pte Ltd and Jorge Santillan c/o Beehive Illustration Agency
Picture research by Susannah Jayes

The author and publishers would like to thank the following for permission to reproduce their photographs:
123rf.com/smileus p106; **Alamy**/Blend Images p65(cm), Alamy/dalekhelen p71(cr), Alamy/Elvele Images Limited p124(tr), Alamy/Gabbro p2, Alamy/Mauritius Images GmbH p104, Alamy/Newscom p87(br), Alamy/Coco Robicheaux p86(cr), Alamy/Rubberball p55, Alamy/sciencephotos p39; **DigitalVision** p24(snake, grasshopper); **Getty Images** p56(iron), Getty Images/akesak p6(br), Getty Images/AndreAnita p80(lion), Getty Images/artisteer p100, Getty Images/BaloOm Studios p24(crab), Getty Images/Martin Barraud p105, Getty Images/Buddy Bartelsen/ullstein bild via Getty Images p122, Getty Images/Anthony Bradshaw p56(gold), Getty Images/Júnior Braz p77(br), Getty Images/bshphotography p48, Getty Images/Caiaimage/Robert Daly p30, Getty Images/Coprid p50(br), Getty Images/Cylonphoto p90(cr), Getty Images/PeterDazeley p6(tr), Getty Images/DEA Picture Library p4(tr), Getty Images/Julie Dermansky/Corbis via Getty Images p87(tr), Getty Images/Frank Deschandol & Philippe Sabine p79(D), Getty Images/Design Pics RF/Array pp68(br), 75(br), Getty Images/DigitalVision p12, Getty Images/Pablo Dolsan/EyeEm p79(C), Getty Images/DuffB p44, Getty Images/Jan-Luc van Eijk/Buiten-beeld/Minden Pictures p83, Getty Images/FatCamera p117(cr), Getty Images/FeodorKorolevsky p63(A), Getty Images/Rene Frederick p117(tr), Getty Images/georgeclerk p41(cr), Getty Images/GMVozd p89(cr), Getty Images/GregorBister p89(tr), Getty Images/Gudella p78(C), Getty Images/Hero Images p20(cr), Getty Images/Jeff Hunter p76, Getty Images/ImagesBazaar p9, Getty Images/iStockphoto/mddphoto p80(giraffe), Getty Images/iStockphoto/Thinkstock/Ammit p50(tr), Getty Images/iStockphoto/Thinkstock Images/ivkuzim p124(tm), Getty Images/iStockphoto/Thinkstock Images/pigphoto p80(tiger), Getty Images/Marc Jackson p65(cr), Getty Images/JasonOndreicka p81(A, D), Getty Images/Roland Jehle/EyeEm p80(tree1), Getty Images/Junghyun Photo p80(tree2), Getty Images/Bradley Kanaris p86(tr), Getty Images/Dorling Kindersley pp49(tr), 78(B), 123(cr), Getty Images/Dave King p92, Getty Images/Christian Kober p85(br), Getty Images/Tibor Kranjec/EyeEm p78(A), Getty Images/Ashish Kumar/EyeEm p29(tr), Getty Images/kuritafsheen p23(stick insect), Getty Images/Bernhard Lang p101, Getty Images/© Ian Laker Photography p74(cr), Getty Images/Leemage p35, Getty Images/lisegagne p29(cr), Getty Images/Ken Lucas p75(tr), Getty Images/Robert Manella p20(cm), Getty Images/Joe McDonald p11, Getty Images/miadn61 p46, Getty Images/MOAimage p74(tr), Getty Images/molefranz p23(crab), Getty Images/DarrenMower p123(tm), Getty Images/nevodka p38(bl), Getty Images/Clive Nichols p71(tr), Getty Images/tam_odin p63(B), Getty Images/Jose Luis Pelaez p14, Getty Images/picturesd p84(tr), Getty Images/Sirintra Pumsopa p62(br), Getty Images/Ridofranz p2, Getty Images/Riccardo Savi p24(wolf), Getty Images/Elisabeth Schmidbauer p29(br), Getty Images/Johann Schumacher p124(cm), Getty Images/Science & Society Picture Library p60(cr), Getty Images/Paul Souders p74(tcr), Getty Images/stamp p67, Getty Images/Stockbyte p95, Getty Images/John Taylor/EyeEm p33(tr), Getty Images/Thinkstock Images/DigitalVision p73(cr), Getty Images/Tuan Tran p25, Getty Images/Анатолий Тушенцов p69(tr), Getty Images/videophoto p38(bl), Getty Images/Xulio Villarino p85(cr), Getty Images/Visuals Unlimited p60(tr), Getty Images/Simon Watson p28, Getty Images/Roberto Westbrook p22, Getty Images/Westend61 p119, Getty Images/AJ Wilhelm p5(cr), Getty Images/Walter Zerla p34; **Image Source** p56(steel); **PhotoDisc** pp109, 124(tr), PhotoDisc/Getty Images p118; **REX Shutterstock**/Nicholas Bailey p97, REX Shutterstock/Bournemouth News p3; **Shutterstock**/Africa Studio p90(tr), Shutterstock/agl100 p63(C), Shutterstock/aharad p23(spider), Shutterstock/Hodyachaya Alla p8(bl), Shutterstock/Alohaflaminggo p42, Shutterstock/axily p73(b), Shutterstock/Bezzangi p62(tr), Shutterstock/Viktor Birkus p19, Shutterstock/Steve Byland p77(cr), Shutterstock/Edwin Godinho p80(impala), Shutterstock/Innershadows Photography p41(cm), Shutterstock/irin-k p79(A), Shutterstock/Matt Jeppson p81(B, C), Shutterstock/jerrysa p36(br), Shutterstock/JohnatAPW p68(cm), Shutterstock/Jouke van Keulen p123(tr), Shutterstock/Sebastian Kaulitzki p5(tr), Shutterstock/James Laurie p79(B), Shutterstock/kb-photodesign p49(br), Shutterstock/basant malviya p96(bl), Shutterstock/Anatoly Maslennikov p64, Shutterstock/Peter Morley p40, Shutterstock/Nixx Photography p72, Shutterstock/Kotomiti Okuma p56(copper), Shutterstock/Photoprofi30 p8(tr), Shutterstock/Alexander Prokopenko p38(tr), Shutterstock/ptnphoto p36(bl), Shutterstock/Darren Pullman p99, Shutterstock/rainyrf p84(b), Shutterstock/Kei Shooting p47(cr, bcr), Shutterstock/sippakom p5(tm), Shutterstock/somchaij p33(br), Shutterstock/senee sriyota p36(cr), Shutterstock/Erik Steinebach p69(cr), Shutterstock/Aleksey Stemmer p23(beetle), Shutterstock/Marcus Stevens p74(cl), Shutterstock/sunsetman p89(br), Shutterstock/Vikulin p45, Shutterstock/Piotr Wytrazek p96(br); **Springer Nature Ltd**/Paul Bricknell p4(bl); **Stockbyte** pp57, 110.

Printed and bound in Brazil
2024
19

Contents

Introducing *Max Science primary*

Max Science primary is a science course designed to meet the needs of learners following the Cambridge International Primary curriculum framework for Stages 1 to 6.

Success in science learning for young international learners and their teachers is enhanced through its practical approach to the skills of scientific enquiry and scientific vocabulary. Investigation and language activities in each unit progress learners from simple to more complex to make learning and understanding science accessible and fun.

The **Student Books** guide learners through key scientific knowledge, language and skills in the Cambridge curriculum. Each unit begins with an engaging introduction followed by activities that introduce and reinforce the skills of scientific enquiry providing opportunities for learners to develop subject knowledge through investigation.

The **Workbooks** expand the key activities in each unit for use by the learners in pairs and groups in the classroom, or as individuals at home.

To further support the course, each stage has a **Journal** for use by learners at home, with the support of adults, to reinforce the knowledge and language of each topic. Teachers can review Journals at different points throughout the term to check progress at home against progress in school.

Also available are ***Max Science primary* Digital Student Books**, which offer an accompaniment to the more traditional printed Student Books. Ideal for encouraging digital literacy, these online books mirror the print course while offering extra interactive activities and assessment opportunities at home or in class.

Student Book features

Unit openers

Introduce the unit with clearly defined learning objectives, and stimulate interest with starter questions and images.

Orientation

Starter activities engage learners and help teachers assess how much the class already knows, before exploring further.

Key words

Key words for each section are clearly shown.

Interesting facts

Link science in the classroom to science in the real world.

Exploring science

Investigations and extension questions help develop skills and understanding, and enable learners to explore, test, measure, record, interpret and predict scientific questions.

Workbook icon

Workbook icons in the Student Book direct teachers and learners to the corresponding activities in the Workbook.

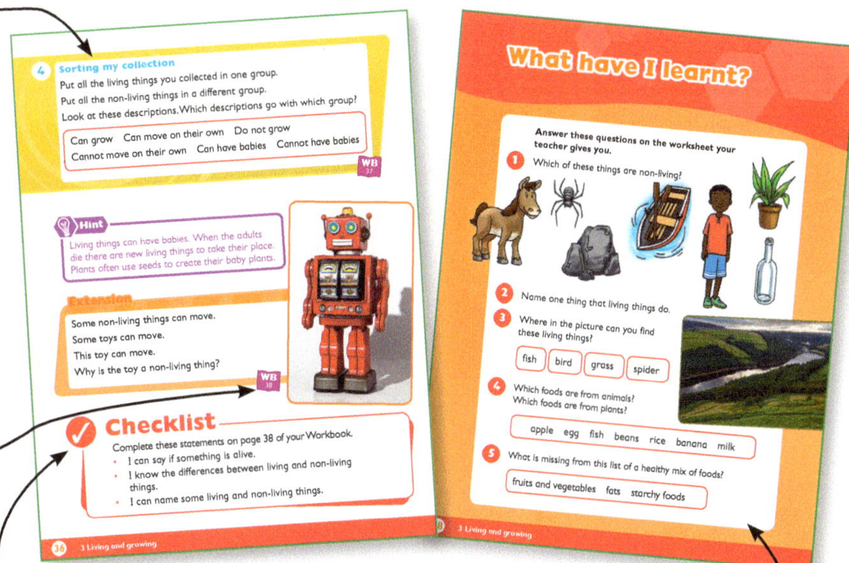

Assessing progress

End of topic checklists allow learners to check what they have learnt so far.

Cambridge Primary curriculum framework

In the spirit of the Cambridge Primary curriculum checkpoint tests, end of unit activities ask 'what have I learnt?' to sum up where learners have got to in their learning journey so far.*

*See *also* the online versions at www.macmillaneducationeverywhere.com for downloading and printing with answer spaces provided.

1 Skeleton and muscles

In this unit, I am learning:

- that our skeleton is made up of bones
- about the main jobs of the skeleton
- how the skeleton grows and moves
- how muscles and bones work together for movement
- about the role of drugs as medicines
- that there are different types of skeleton.

Key words

animal
contract
fracture
invertebrate
muscles
relax
skeleton
vertebrate
X-ray

What are the children doing? What helps them to move their bodies? How do they keep their bodies upright?

1.1 Skeletons

In this section, I am learning:

- that bones form our skeleton
- about X-ray images.

Key words

animal, bones, discuss, fingers, fracture, human, skeleton, vertebrate, X-ray

What can the children find out from looking at these old bones?

Skeletons can tell us secrets

Many **animals** have bones inside their bodies. Animals with bones inside their bodies are called **vertebrates**.

The **bones** form a **skeleton**.

Bones are hard. They exist for a long time after an animal has died.

Dinosaurs lived millions of years ago. No one has ever seen a living dinosaur. Scientists called palaeontologists look at dinosaur bones to get an idea of what these animals looked like.

Hint

Think about how dinosaurs moved. What do you think they ate? How did they fight?

1 Drawing the dinosaurs

a. Look at the picture of a dinosaur skeleton. Imagine what the dinosaurs looked like when they were alive. **Discuss** your ideas with your partner.

b. Draw a picture in your Workbook.

WB 1

The picture shows a bone from the leg of a dinosaur called *Diplodocus*. It is 160 cm long.

By looking at the bones, palaeontologists worked out that *Diplodocus* must have stood about 8 m high.

What *Diplodocus* may have looked like

Extension

Look at some more pictures of dinosaur skeletons. What clues do the skeletons give about how dinosaurs lived?

WB 1

2 Investigating bones

Get into groups. Your teacher will give you some bones to examine.

a. What do the bones look like?

b. What do the bones feel like?

c. Choose one of the bones. What part of the animal do you think it comes from?

Note your observations in your Workbook.

WB 2

There are 206 bones in the **human** body. They all do different things.

Interesting fact

There are 27 bones in a human hand.

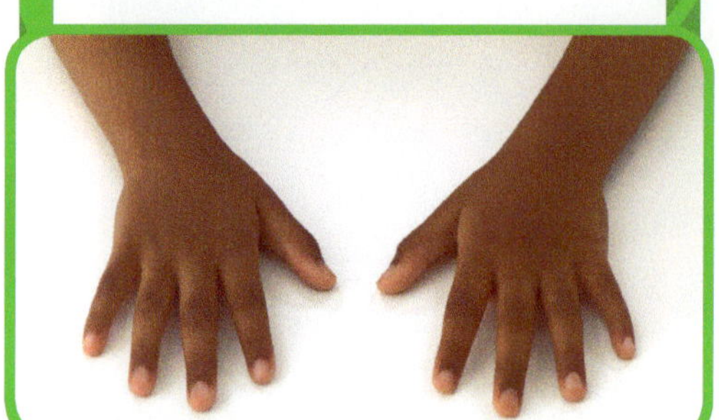

3 Bones and fingers

a. Touch your **fingers**. What can you feel under the skin?

b. Now bend your fingers. Try to count the bones in each finger.

c. In your Workbook, draw a picture of what you think your finger skeleton looks like.

WB 3

Understanding our skeleton

Many of the bones in our skeleton look similar to those of other animals, although animal bones may be bigger or smaller than ours.

dog skeleton

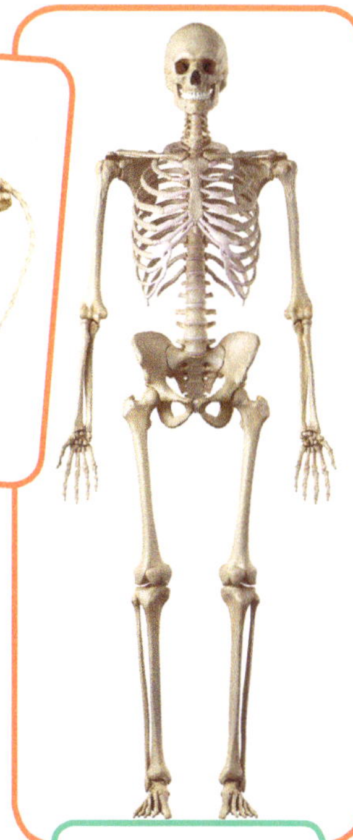

human skeleton

The human skeleton stands upright. This is different from the skeletons of other animals.

Look at the pictures.

In what ways are the two skeletons similar? How are they different? Talk to your partner.

Evidence from X-rays

In a hospital, a health worker called a radiographer can take an **X-ray** image of your bones.

When the X-ray image is taken the radiographer has to stand behind a special screen to protect themselves. X-rays can be dangerous if you are exposed to them for a long period. A radiographer can take many X-ray images every day.

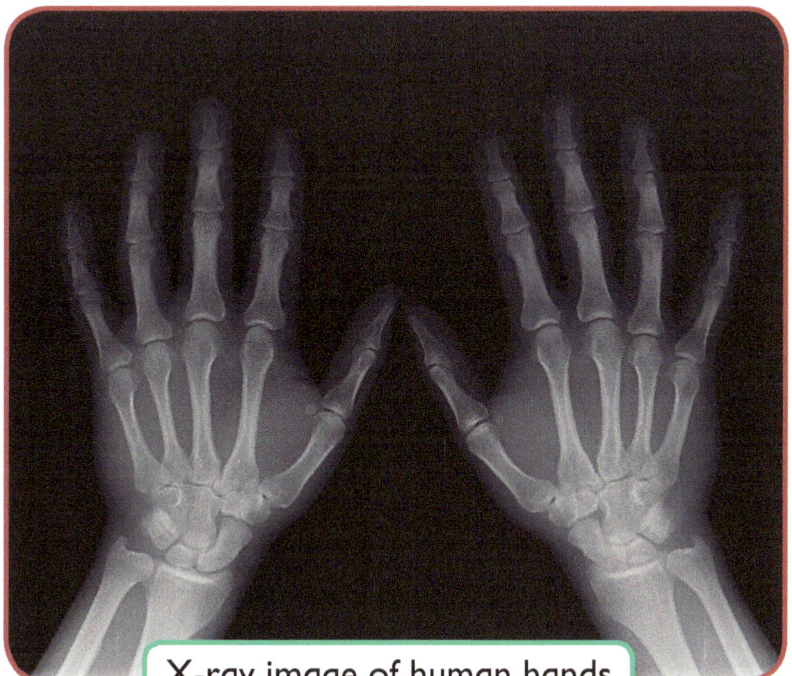

X-ray image of human hands

Why do you think X-ray images are useful? Discuss your ideas with your partner.

4 Getting an X-ray image

Pretend that someone in your group has broken their arm.

They need to have an X-ray image taken.

Role play what happens at the hospital.

WB 3

If a bone is broken, we say it has a **fracture**. We can see a bone fracture on an X-ray image.

How can you tell which bone is fractured?

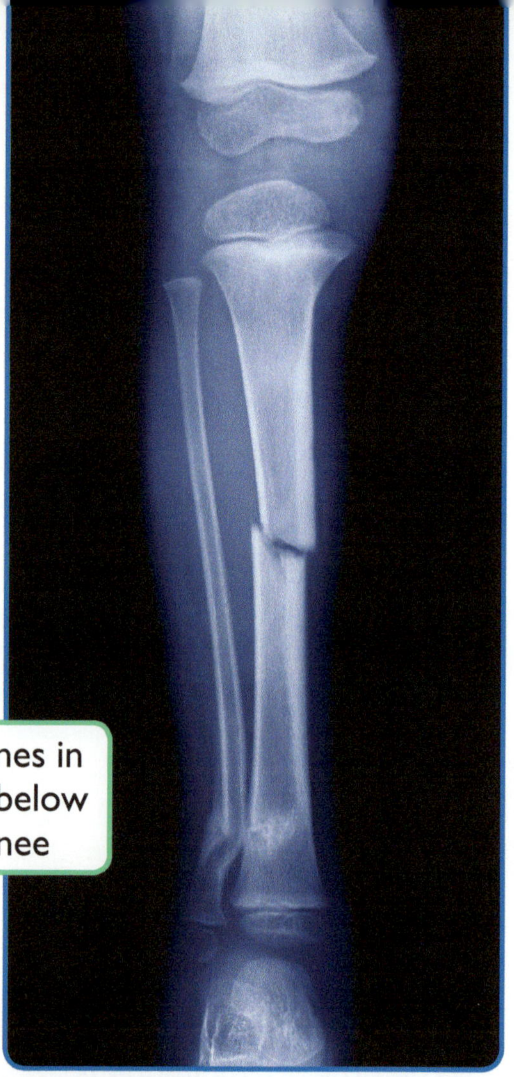

Interesting fact

If you fracture a bone, it can usually grow and heal again. Sometimes a pin is used to hold the broken parts together as they heal.

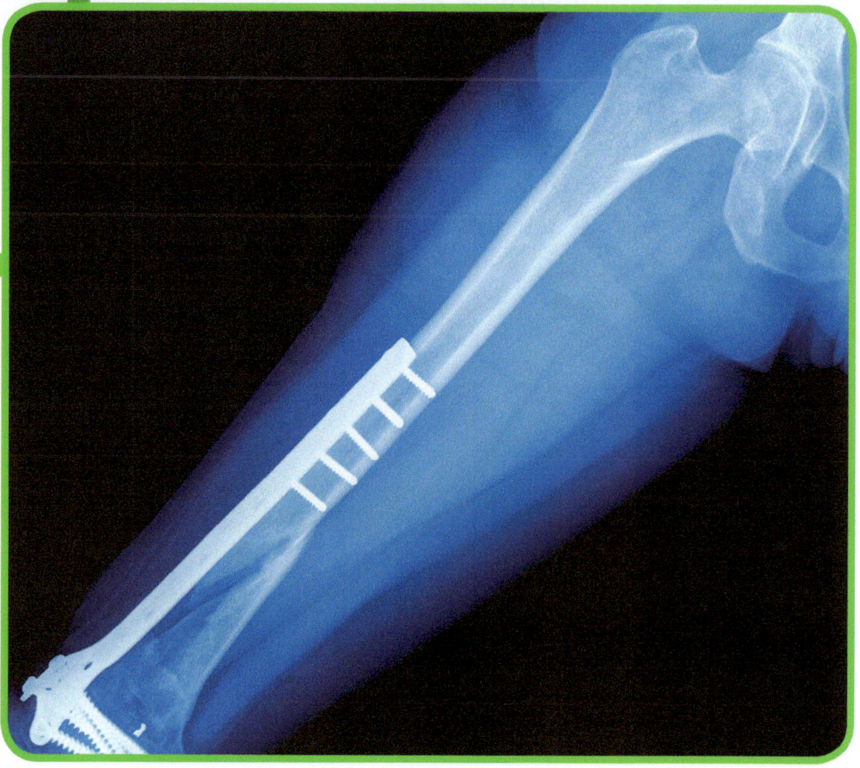

1.2 The human skeleton

Key words

ankle
compare
feet
knee
name
ribs
shoulders
spine
thumbs
wrist
arm
elbow
hip
move
neck
shin
skull
thigh
vertebrae

In this section, I am learning:

- about the jobs of the skeleton
- to recognise and name parts of the human skeleton.

The human skeleton

Without a skeleton, your body would not have any structure. You would not be able to stand upright or move around.

Look at the labelled diagram of the human skeleton. Can you find the different bones in your own body?

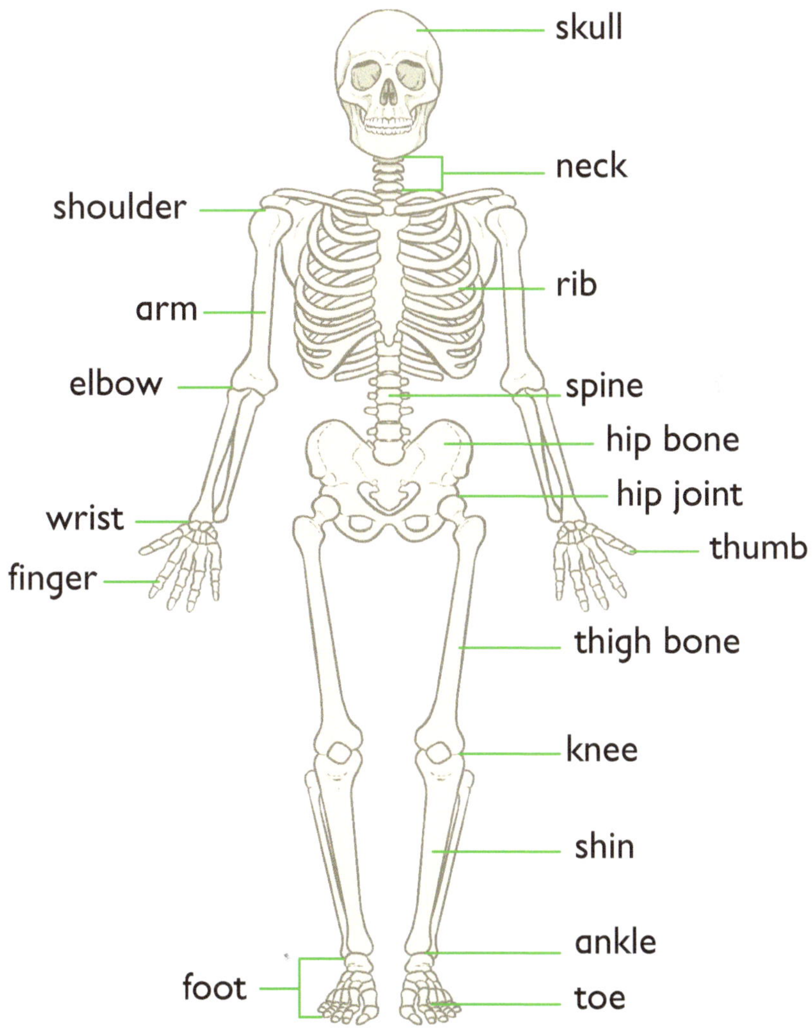

human skeleton

The skeleton protects vital organs

Bones are hard and strong. The **ribs** and **skull** surround vital organs such as the heart, lungs and brain.

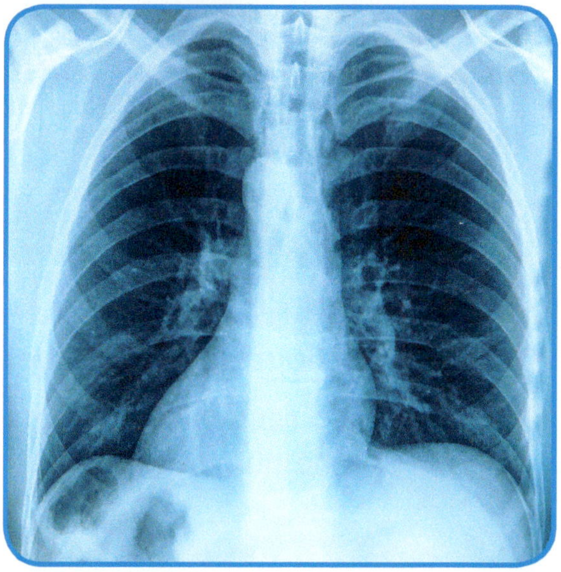

Our skeleton helps us to move

The place where two bones connect is called a joint. Joints allow us to **move** parts of our body.

There is a joint between the bones in your upper and lower **arm**. We call this the **elbow**.

What would happen if you did not have an elbow joint?

Your **hip** is also a type of joint. It connects the bone in your **thigh** to your upper body.

The hip allows you to move your legs in different ways.

How does your hip let you move your leg? How is it different from what your elbow does?

The thigh bone above the knee is the strongest and largest bone in your body.

The part of your leg below the knee has two bones. The front one is called your **shin**.

Your **knee** connects the thigh bone to the bones below your knee. The knee is also a joint.

Talk about how your knees allow your legs to move.

There are 26 bones in each of your **feet**.

How do the bones in your feet compare with the bones in your hand, which you felt earlier?

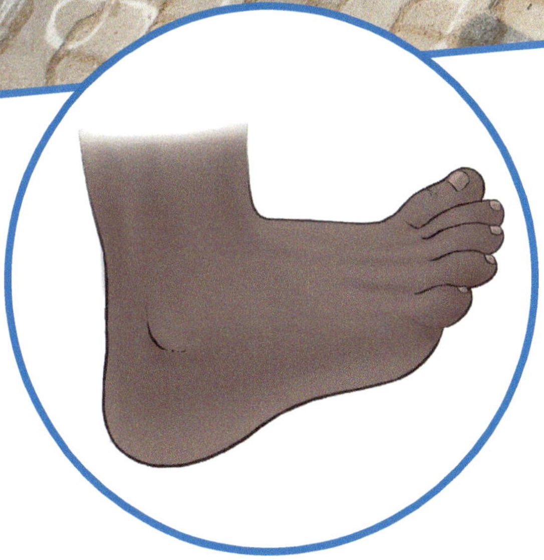

The joint just above your foot is your **ankle**.

How do your ankles allow your feet to move?

The joint that connects the bones of your hand to your arm is called the **wrist**.

Compare your wrist and your ankle. Do the joints work in the same way?

Your **thumbs** can move outwards and inwards. They allow you to grip things.

Our skeleton supports the body

Bones form the structure to which muscles connect.

Your **spine** keeps you upright. It is made up of many short, wide bones, called **vertebrae**. The first seven vertebrae of the spine form your **neck**. Your neck links your **shoulders** to your head.

Would you be able to move like this if your spine was just one long bone?

In what other ways can you move your back?

There are joints between your vertebrae. They help you to bend your back and move your neck.

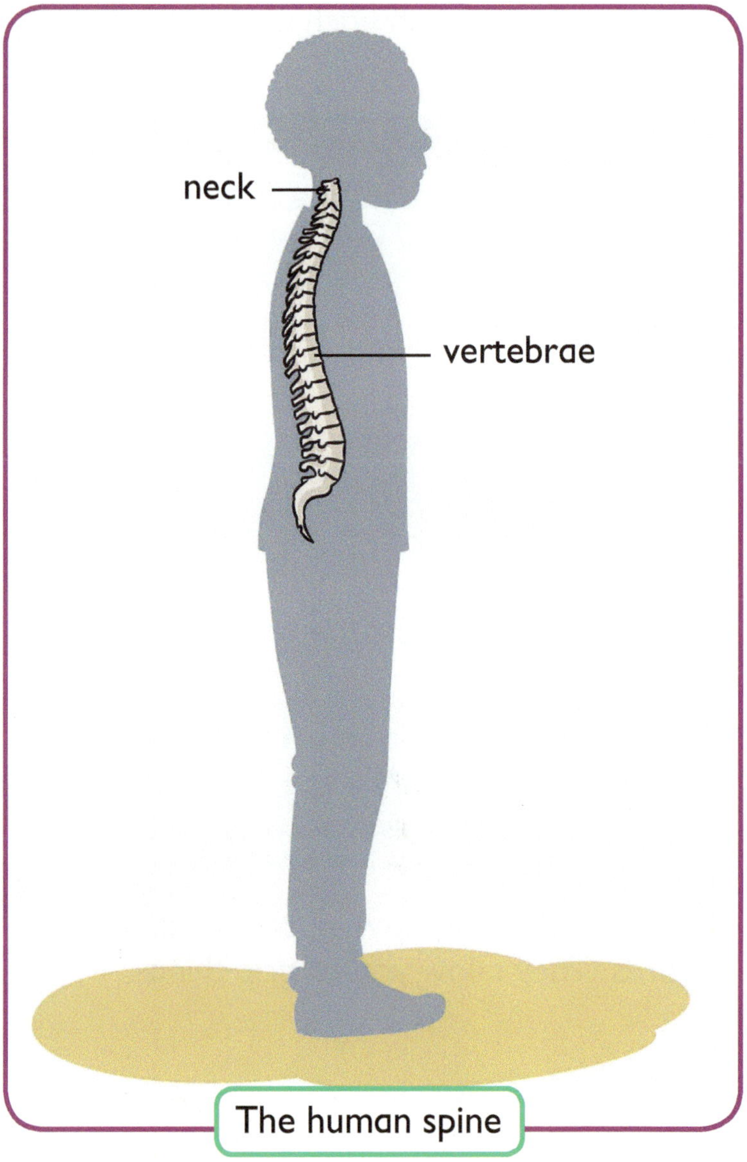

The human spine

1 Muddled skeleton

Hakim was not at school when his class learnt about the human skeleton.

He has got the bones all muddled.

Can you help him?

WB 4

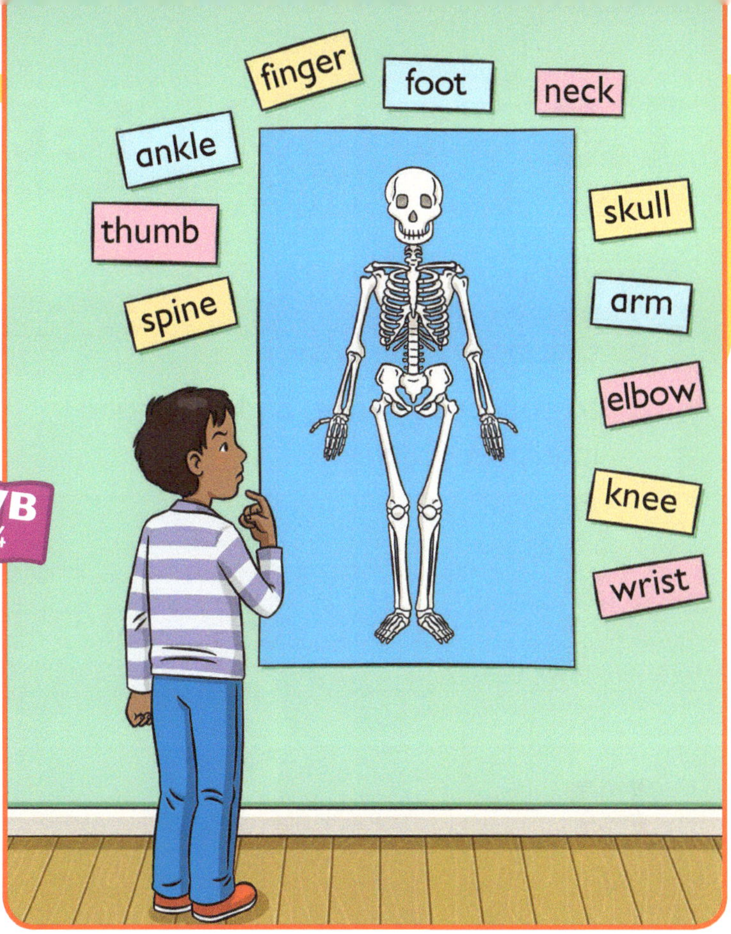

Extension

a. How does the skeleton protect the brain, heart and lungs?

b. Why do these organs need protection?

WB 5

2 What jobs does the skeleton do?

The three main jobs of the skeleton are support, protection and movement.

a. Find the names of nine bones hidden among the letters in your Workbook.

b. Which jobs do the bones do?

WB 5

Interesting fact

An adult human skeleton has 206 bones. A snake skeleton has more than 500 bones.

1.3 Do skeletons grow?

In this section, I am learning:

- that bones can grow
- to collect evidence, and draw and interpret graphs.

Key words

collect, conclusion, evidence, measure, patterns, predict, results, trend

Look at these skeletons. How are they similar? How are they different? Discuss your ideas with your partner.

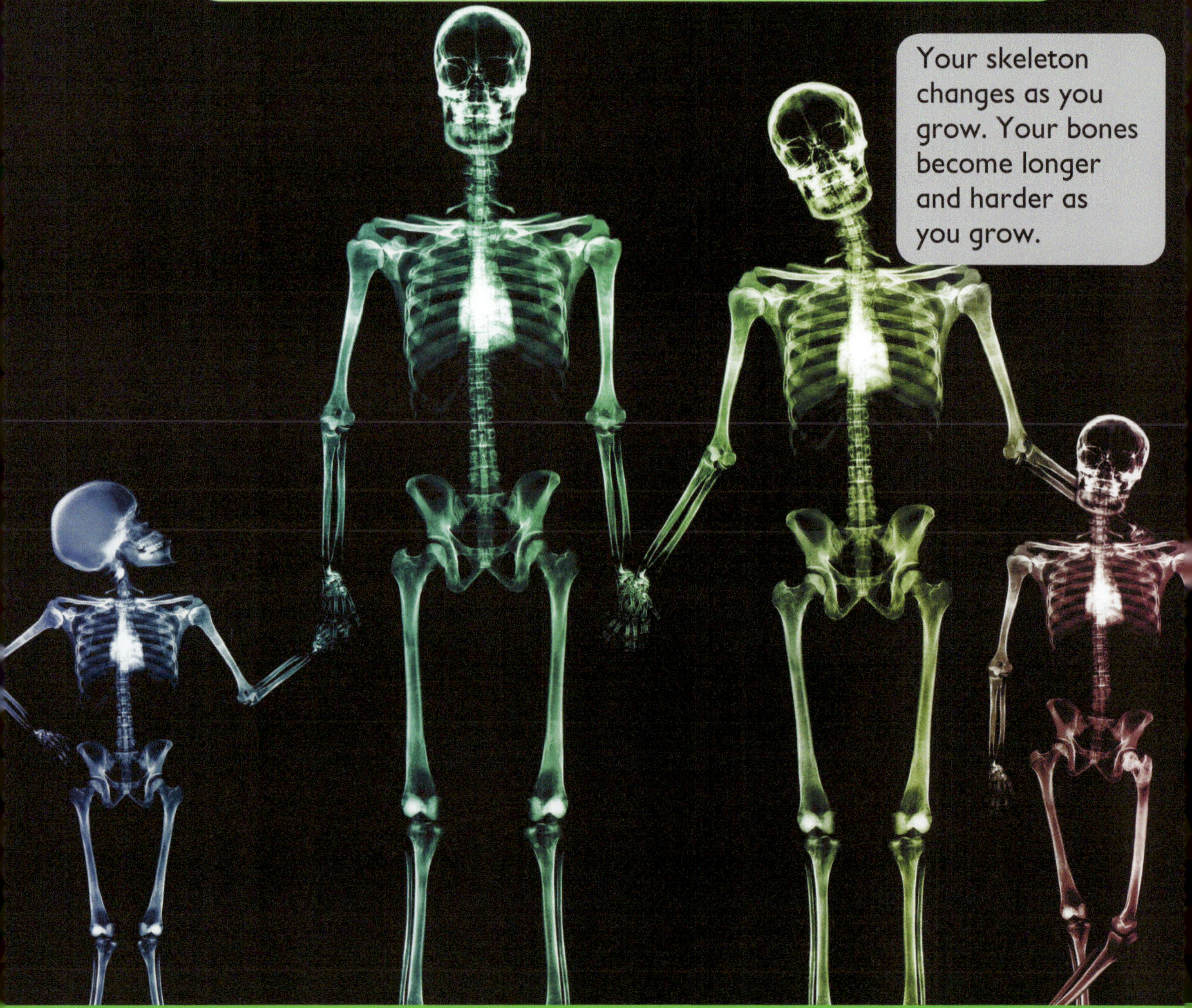

We can measure how long our bones are. Doctors measure the length of children's bones to see if they are growing well.

1 Investigating bone lengths

Work with a partner.
Use a ruler to **measure** your arm bones.

a. How long is the bone in your lower arm?

b. Is it the same length as other people's bones?

c. Look at all the measurements in the class. What pattern can you see?

WB 6

Extension

a. Measure the bones of some adults and younger children. **Collect** some **results**.

b. What can you learn from your measurements?

c. Can you use your measurements as **evidence** that bones can grow?

WB 7

A graph, like a bar chart, can help us to compare measurements.

2 Drawing a bar chart

Look at the measurements in your Workbook.

a. Draw a bar chart to compare the measurements.

b. What **patterns** can you see? Is there a **trend**?

c. What **conclusions** can you make?

WB 8

Interesting fact

A baby is born with about 300 bones. As the baby grows and develops, many of the smaller bones join up and fuse together.

How do skeletons change over time?

Your bones are living. They are made from a substance called calcium.

Calcium is found in dairy foods such as milk, yoghurt and cheese. Eating dairy foods helps your bones to grow and become strong and healthy.

Do your bones keep on growing all your life?

Hint

Children need to drink more milk than adults.

Changes in bone length

The thigh bone goes from your hip to your knee.

Extension

a. When do you think our bones stop growing?

b. Why is this important?

c. Matin is 40 years old. Can you **predict** which thigh bone belongs to him?

d. Draw the bones in order of people's ages. What pattern do you see?

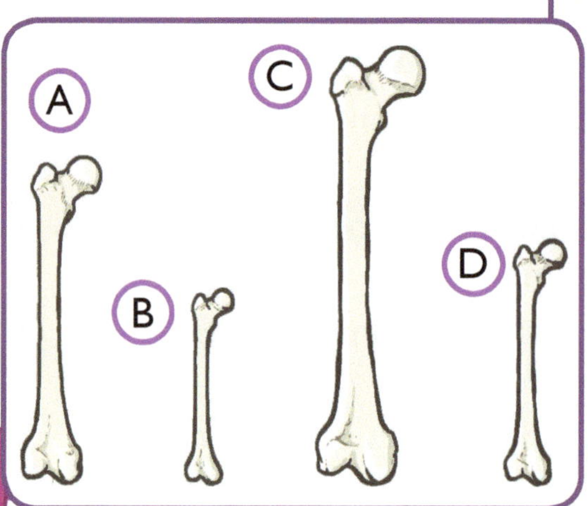

WB 9

The chart shows the average length of a human thigh bone at different ages. The bone grows longer until we become adults.

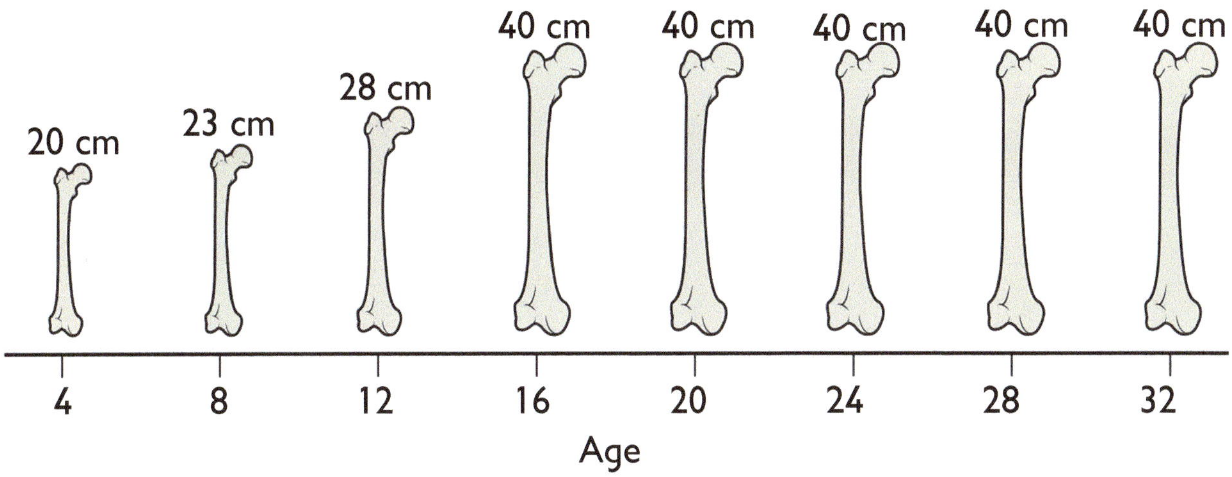

Growth of human thigh bone

3 Growth of the human thigh bone

Use the chart to answer the following questions.

a. How long is the thigh bone of someone who is 12 years old?

b. How long do you think the thigh bone will be for someone who is:
- 9 years old?
- 40 years old?

c. In which four-year period does the thigh bone grow the most?

d. What general trend can you see in the results?

WB 10

Checklist

Complete these statements on page 11 of your Workbook.

- I know that our skeleton consists of many different bones.
- I know that X-ray images can show us how our bones look.
- I know what the three jobs of my skeleton are.
- I can name parts of the human skeleton.
- I know that my bones grow with my body and can heal if they break.

1.4 What are medicines?

In this section, I am learning:

- how medicines can help to make us better
- that medicines can be dangerous if not taken correctly
- to name some common medicines.

Key words
cure
medicine
suggest
symptoms

Have you ever been ill? What did it feel like? What did you do to get better?

Different types of medicine

When we are ill, we feel unwell. The signs of illness our body shows are called **symptoms**. A tummy ache is a symptom. A fever is a symptom. Losing your appetite is a symptom.

1 Treatments for symptoms

Work with your partner. How can you help someone who is not feeling well?

In your Workbook, match each symptom to the action you think is best.

WB 12

When you feel unwell, getting rest, staying warm, eating food and drinking enough water can help.

But sometimes it is not enough. Then we may need to take **medicine** to help us get better.

There are many different types of medicine. They can help us feel better or **cure** our illness.

It is important to take the correct medicine, and the correct amount. It can be very dangerous to take the wrong type or the wrong amount of medicine.

Safety

Always ask an adult before taking any medicine.

2 Which medicine?

Look at the medicines your teacher shows you.

a. Which of these medicines have you taken?

b. Why did you take the medicine? What were your symptoms?

c. Which other medicines do you remember taking?

Share your stories about medicines with your class.

WB 12–13

All medicines come with an information leaflet. This gives important advice about:

- what the medicine is used for
- who should take the medicine
- how to take the medicine.

3 Be safe with medicines

Look at the information leaflet for aspirin.

a. Read the information carefully. Why is it important to do so?

b. Answer the questions in your Workbook about taking this medicine.

Medicine = Aspirin

Used for: Headaches, symptoms of cold and flu, fever, sore throat, toothache

Contains: Aspirin

Warning: Do not give to children under 16 years old, unless advised by a doctor.

How to take: Take 1 to 3 tablets every 4 hours. Do not take more than 12 tablets in 24 hours.

Do not take aspirin if you:

- have stomach ulcers
- are younger than 16
- are allergic to aspirin or any substances included.

Each tablet contains: 300 mg aspirin, maize starch, talc, lemon flavour and sweetener.

WB 13–14

Extension

The label on a bottle of a cough medicine for children says:

> **Children aged 6 – 12 years: Take 2.5 ml (½ teaspoon) twice a day.**
>
> **Do not take more than 5 ml (1 teaspoon) in 24 hours.**

Jacob is 8 years old. He has a cough. His mother gave him 2.5 ml of medicine at 10 O'clock in the morning.

At 5 O'clock in the afternoon, Jacob is still feeling unwell. Can his mother give him more medicine?

WB 14

Interesting fact

Reports say that in the US, doctors in the emergency rooms of hospitals treat a child for taking the wrong medicine, or taking it incorrectly, every 8 minutes.

4 School rules for anyone feeling unwell

Have you ever felt unwell in school? What did you do? Who did you talk to?

a. Find out the rules for your school.

b. What do you suggest to improve these rules?

WB 15

Checklist

Complete these statements on page 15 of your Workbook.

- I know that there are different types of medicine.
- I know that medicine can help to make us better when we are ill.
- I know that all medicines can be dangerous if taken incorrectly.
- I can say what kind of information is given in an information leaflet.
- I know that children may take medicine only when an adult is present.

1.5 Movement, bones and muscles

In this section, I am learning:

- how the skeleton brings about movement
- how bones and muscles work together.

Key words

apparatus	contract
equipment	factor
fair test	muscles
relax	variables

You already know that your skeleton helps your body to move. The bones of your skeleton have **muscles** attached to them. Muscles make it possible for bones to move.

Look at the pictures. Which bones are moving? How do you think the muscles work to help the bones to move?

What are muscles?

Muscles are long elastic fibres. They can **contract**, which means they can become shorter. They can also **relax**, which means that they can return to their original length. Bones can move at joints when our muscles contract or relax.

1 Moving in different ways

a. Move your body in different ways. Which bones or joints are you using in each movement?

- Nod your head.
- Wiggle your toes.
- Move your shoulders and your hips.

b. How do your muscles help to make the bones move?

WB 16

Muscles that work in pairs

Some muscles work in pairs. Examples are the muscles in your upper arm and leg.

When you bend your arm, the muscle in the front of your upper arm contracts. The muscle at the back of your upper arm relaxes.

The two muscles work in opposite ways. The muscle that contracts becomes shorter. The muscle that relaxes is long. The two muscles work together as a pair.

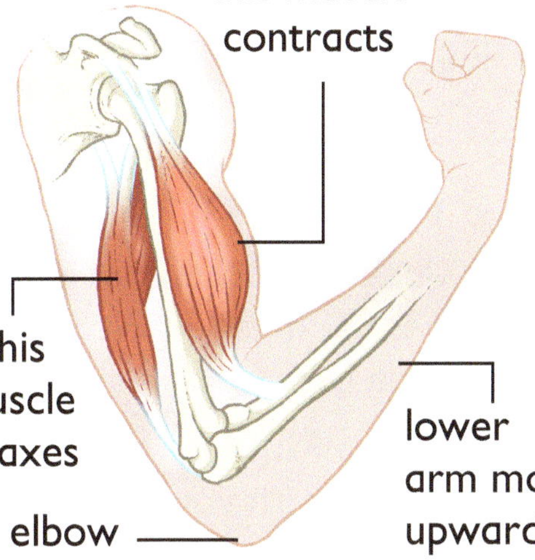

A pair of muscles work together to make the elbow joint move.

2 How do bones move?

Watch a video about how muscles and bones work together.

Then get into groups.

a. Make a model of how your muscles and elbow let you move your arm.

b. Describe how the model works.

WB 17

Your leg muscles change shape as you move your leg. You can feel your muscles moving.

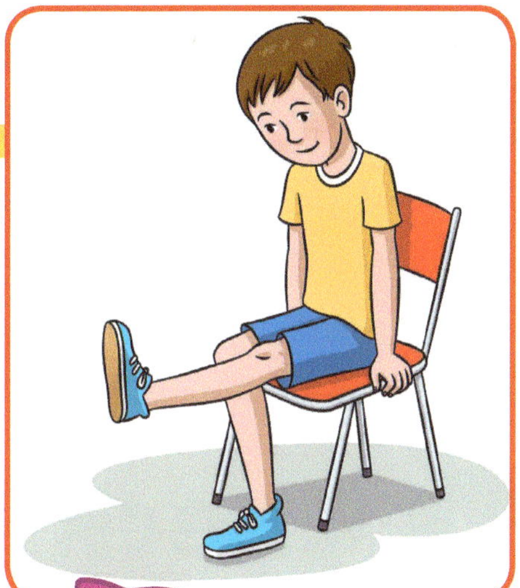

3 Exploring leg muscles

Sit on a chair, with your legs bent. Lift up your lower leg.

a. How do the muscles in the front of your thigh change during the movement?

b. How do the muscles at the back of your thigh change during the movement?

Write your observations in your Workbook.

WB 18

Extension

You have learnt about bones and muscles. How do they work together?

Complete the sentences in your Workbook.

WB 18

Exercise can make our muscles stronger. Strong muscles can lift heavy things.

4 Investigating muscles

Jack and Bill are weight lifters. Jack has big muscles. He says he is stronger than Bill.

Plan a **fair test** to see if Jack is right. Work with your partner.

Answer these questions to help you plan your test.

a. What are the **variables**?

b. Which **factor** will you change?

c. What will you measure?

d. What **apparatus** or **equipment** will you need?

WB 19

Interesting fact

You have more than 600 skeletal muscles in your body. To take a step, you use muscles across your whole body.

Checklist

Complete these statements on page 19 of your Workbook.

- I know that muscles are attached to my skeleton.
- I can describe how muscles work in pairs to make my bones move.
- I can describe how muscles relax and contract.

1.6 Other types of skeleton

In this section, I am learning:

- about invertebrates
- how the skeletons of vertebrates and invertebrates are different.

Key words
invertebrate
observe
vertebrate

Animals without bony skeletons

You learnt earlier that animals with a skeleton inside their body are **vertebrates**. Vertebrates have a backbone. Humans are vertebrates.

Animals such as beetles, insects, spiders and crabs do not have a skeleton inside their body. They do not have a backbone. We say these animals are **invertebrates**.

stick insect

spider

beetle

crab

Look at the photos of invertebrates.

What gives their bodies structure if they do not have a bony skeleton inside?

Discuss your ideas with your partner.

1 Observing invertebrates

a. Go on a tour around your school grounds.
Look for some invertebrates. They might be in the soil or under stones.

b. Use a magnifying glass to **observe** the invertebrates. Record your observations in your Workbook.

WB 20–21

Safety

Be careful when handling invertebrates. They are animals and must be respected.

Invertebrates do not have a skeleton inside their body. Some invertebrates have a hard covering outside their body. This is called an **exoskeleton**.

Some invertebrates do not have a skeleton at all, like a jellyfish.

2 Which type of skeleton?

Look at the photos of different animals. What kinds of skeleton can you see?

- Which animals are vertebrates?
- Which animals are invertebrates with an exoskeleton?
- Which animals have no skeleton at all?

WB 21–22

Comparing the movement of vertebrates and invertebrates

Invertebrates and vertebrates move in different ways. A crab is an invertebrate. It does not move in the same way as a vertebrate animal such as a wolf.

Which animal is likely to have the most joints? Which animal is likely to have the most muscles? Which animal do you think moves in a way most different from you?

3 Designing your own invertebrate

Imagine you have discovered a new invertebrate animal.

a. Describe what it looks like.

- What is its outside skeleton like?
- What shape is it?
- What colour is it?

b. Draw this new invertebrate in your Workbook.

c. What are the advantages of an exoskeleton? What are the disadvantages?

WB 22–23

Interesting fact

Of all the animals in the world, 97% are invertebrates.

Extension

Find out more about an invertebrate animal. How does it move? What gives its body support? How does it protect its softer parts?

Prepare a short talk for your class.

WB 23

✓ Checklist

Complete these statements on page 23 of your Workbook.

- I know what the difference is between a vertebrate and an invertebrate animal.
- I can name some vertebrate and invertebrate animals.
- I can compare different types of skeleton.

What have I learnt?

Answer these questions on the worksheet your teacher gives you.

1. What are the three main jobs of the skeleton?

2. Describe what the word 'fracture' means.

3. Are these statements true or false?
   - **a.** All animals have a skeleton.
   - **b.** The skeletons of vertebrates are all the same.
   - **c.** Muscles that work in pairs both contract at the same time.

4. Complete the sentences using the words from the box.

vertebrae	lungs	skull	heart	joints	neck

The ____ protects the brain. It is attached to the ____. The bones in the neck and spine are called ____. The ribs protect the ____ and ____. The elbow and knee are ____. They allow more flexible movements.

5. Explain how the pair of muscles in your upper arm works when you bend your elbow.

   Use the words 'relax' and 'contract' in your explanation. Draw a diagram to help you.

6. What important information will you find in a medicine leaflet?

7. How is the skeleton of an invertebrate different from the skeleton of a vertebrate?

8. Which part of the skeleton enables us to move in many different ways?

2 Solids, liquids and gases

Key words
boil
freeze
gas
liquid
matter
melt
particles
solid
temperature

In this unit, I am learning:

- to recognise solids, liquids and gases
- that solids, liquids and gases are three states of matter
- how the particle model describes each of these three states of matter
- how heating affects solids and liquids
- how cooling affects liquids and gases
- to measure temperature using a thermometer.

What is happening in the picture? Describe what you see.

2.1 Comparing solids, liquids and gases

In this section, I am learning:

- what matter is
- that solid, liquid and gas are the three states of matter
- about the differences between solids, liquids and gases.

Key words

gas, group, liquid, matter, select, solid

Identifying solids, liquids and gases

Everything around us is made of something. Scientists call this **matter**.

Matter takes up space and has weight.

What can you see in these pictures? Is there solid, liquid and gas?

Matter can exist in three forms: **solid**, **liquid** and **gas**. We call these the three states of matter.

1 Features of solids, liquids and gases

What words can we use to describe ice, water and steam?

Think about:

- how it feels to hold an ice cube
- what water feels like
- what steam looks like.

Select words from the list in your Workbook to complete the sentences. You can also add some words of your own.

WB 26

Water can exist in all three states.

The pool of water is a liquid. Steam is a gas. Ice is a solid.

Do all solids look like ice? Do all liquids look like water? Do all gases look like steam? Explain your answers.

Solids, liquids and gases are all around us. Tears are liquid. The air is a gas. Wood is solid.

2 Exploring the properties of solids, liquids and gases

Work in a group.

a. Carry out some tests to investigate the properties of solids, liquids and gases.

b. In your Workbook, write down what properties you found for solids, liquids and gases.

WB 26–27

3 Finding solids, liquids and gases

Look at some materials around your classroom. **Group** them as solids, liquids or gases in your Workbook.

WB 27

Interesting fact

Look at the children throwing leaves into the air. They cannot see or smell the air, but it is there. The air around us is a mixture of gases. Nitrogen and oxygen make up the largest part of air.

2.2 The particle model

In this section, I am learning:

- how a model can represent an idea
- about the particle model for a solid, a liquid and a gas.

Key words

draw
drip
explain
flow
model
particles
predict

Look at the cartoon. What do you think about the children's questions?

Share your ideas with your partner.

A particle model for solids, liquids and gases

Matter is made up of small bits. We call these small bits **particles**. Particles are too small to see except with very special microscopes. We use a **model** to help us understand what the particles of matter are like in different states.

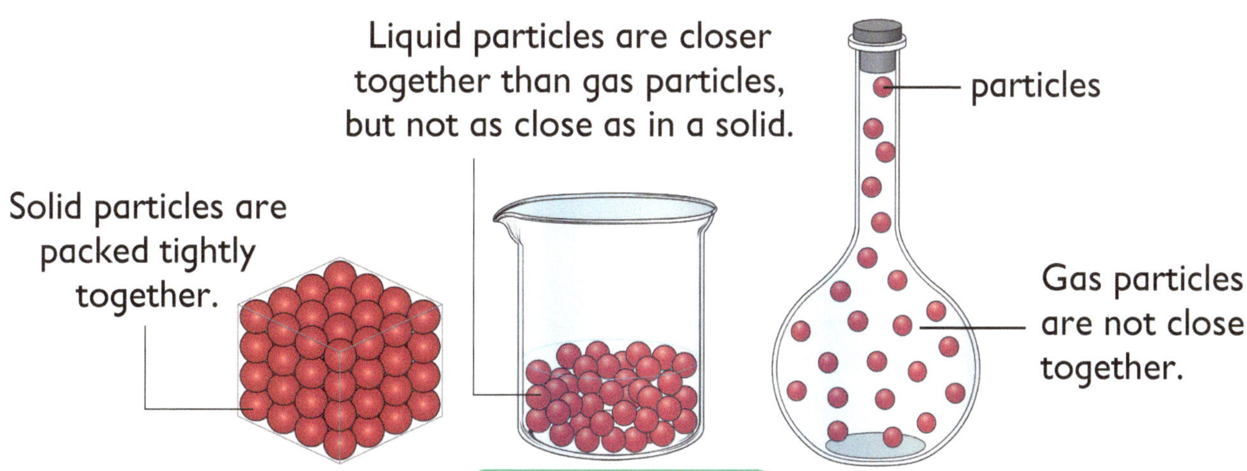

States of matter

Look at the pictures of popcorn. Think of the popcorn as particles of matter.

In which picture does the popcorn behave like a solid, a liquid or a gas?

Particle model for a solid

The particles in a solid are very closely packed, always touching each other. They stay in a fixed position. The particles do not move about, but they can vibrate in their positions. They are in a regular pattern.

1 Acting out a particle model for a solid

People can act like particles.

Get into groups. Imagine you are particles in a solid.

a. Work together to make a people model for a solid.

b. Describe the shape of a solid with your model.

c. Think back to what you observed about the properties of solids earlier. Does your model fit these observations?

WB 28

Hint

Think back to what you found out about the properties of a solid. Are solids hard or soft? Is it easy to pull a solid apart? Can you easily change the shape of a solid?

Particle model for a liquid

The particles in a liquid are arranged more loosely than those in a solid. They still touch, but they do not stay in a fixed position. They move about slowly. Liquids do not have a fixed shape like solids. Liquids can **flow** and take the shape of the container or space they are in.

Why do you think the water in the stream can flow around the rocks? How does the way the particles are arranged help?

2 Acting out a particle model for a liquid

Get into groups again.

a. Try to make a people model of a liquid in a container.

b. Compare the way particles behave in a liquid and a solid if there is no container.

c. How do the particles behave in a liquid when they are squeezed together?

WB 28–29

Extension

Drip some milk and some honey onto a plate.

a. Are they both liquids? Why do you say so?

b. **Predict** what will happen if you warm up the honey. Try to **explain** your answer using what you know about the particle model for liquids.

WB 29

Particle model for a gas

The particles in a gas do not stay still. They move about fast and in different directions. The particles bump into each other, but do not stay in contact for long. There are wide spaces between the particles of a gas.

The bubbles in this drink are a gas.

3 Acting out a particle model for a gas

Get into groups one more time.

a. Imagine you are a particle in a gas. Work with your group to make a people model of a gas.

b. How is your model different from those for a solid or a liquid? Write your ideas in your Workbook.

WB 29–30

We can make drawings of our models to explain our ideas to other people.

4 Comparing particle models for solids, liquids and gases

a. Match the descriptions of particles to the correct state of matter in your Workbook.

b. Use these ideas to **draw** particle models for a solid, a liquid and a gas.

WB 30–31

Hint

Think back to what your people models showed to help you make your drawings.

Different materials have different properties, even if they are in the same state. Cheese and wood are both solids, but they feel different.

Knowing the properties of a material helps us to work with it easily.

Interesting fact

The idea that matter is made up of particles was first thought of by an ancient Greek called Democritus. Democritus lived in Greece about 2500 years ago.

Checklist

Complete these statements on page 31 of your Workbook.

- I can recognise solids, liquids and gases around me.
- I can describe the properties of solids, liquids and gases.
- I can describe how the particles in a solid, liquid and gas are arranged and how they behave.

2.3 Investigating liquids

In this section, I am learning:

- that different liquids have different properties
- to investigate how different liquids flow.

Key words

decide
measure
pattern
pour
powder
repeat
results
table
trend

A property of all liquids is that they can flow. They take the shape of their container. However, not all liquids flow in the same way. Some liquids are runnier than others.

water

Look at the liquids in the pictures.

Which one is the runniest? Which one flows slowest?

How do you know? Talk about it with your partner.

fabric softener

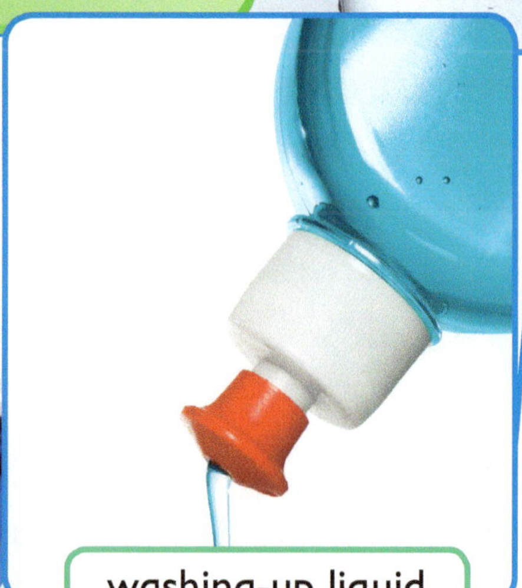

washing-up liquid

olive oil

It can be difficult to tell how runny a liquid is by looking at it. An investigation will give us more accurate **results**.

1 Finding the runniest liquids

Get into groups. Do all liquids flow at the same speed? Your teacher will give you some equipment and different liquids to test.

a. Plan an investigation to find out how fast different liquids can flow.

- What equipment will you use?
- **Decide** how to make it a fair test.
- What will you **measure**?

b. Draw up a **table** for your results.

c. Carry out your investigation.

d. Present your results as a chart. Can you see a **trend**?

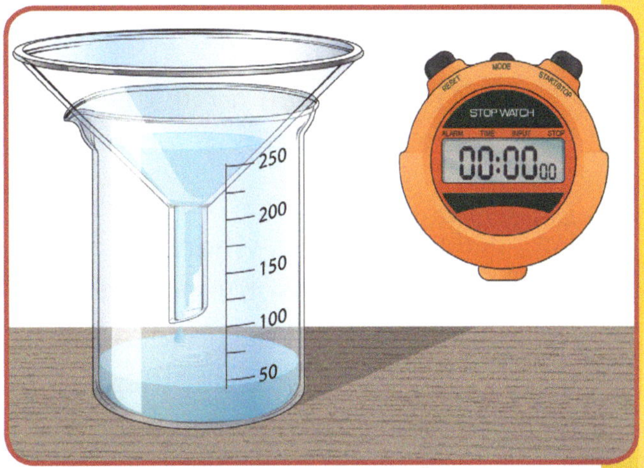

WB 32–34

Hint

A trend is when results show a similar **pattern**.

Look at the picture.

Will the marble move equally fast through the water and the oil?

How thick or thin a liquid is affects how fast it flows. If a liquid is thick, an object will move through it slowly. Thick liquids flow more slowly than thin liquids.

A **powder** is a solid that has been crushed or ground into lots of little pieces. Examples are sand, sugar and salt.

Powders can behave a bit like liquids, but they are still solids.

Sugar is a powder.

2 Investigating pouring

You will need a cup of sand and a cup of water.

a. Observe what happens when you **pour** water onto a dish. Then pour the sand onto another dish. Talk about what happened.

b. How is sand like a liquid? Why? Can you explain why sand is still a solid?

c. Predict what will happen if you **repeat** this with a cup of rice.

WB 35

Interesting fact

Mercury is a shiny, silvery metal. Unlike other metals, mercury is a liquid at room temperature. It turns into a solid only at about −38 °C.

Checklist

Complete these statements on page 35 of your Workbook.

- I can name some liquids that flow easily and some that do not.
- I can describe an investigation to measure how fast liquids flow.
- I can recognise that some solids are unusual and appear to flow.

2.4 Investigating gases

In this section, I am learning:

- about the properties of gases
- how to make a gas in science class.

Key words

bubbles
collect
evidence
record
test

The properties of gases

Gases are not all the same. Some gases are visible but others are not.

Look at the gases in the containers. What do you think gases are like?

Your teacher will demonstrate how to make a cloud of gas in a bottle. Can you see the gas? Where else can you find gas in the room?

Gases themselves can be difficult to see and feel. But we can look for signs of gases around us.

1 Looking for signs of gases

Use the materials your teacher gives or shows you.

What evidence do you have that a gas is present?

Talk about it with your partner. Then write your observations in your Workbook.

WB 36–37

Bubbles show that a gas is present. We can see bubbles in this fizzy drink because a gas has been added to the liquid.

You already know that the particles in a gas move about freely.

If a gas is in a closed container, the particles will move around all the available space in the container. A gas takes the shape of the container it is in.

If the container does not have a lid, the gas will spread out throughout the air around us. To use a gas, we have to contain it.

Balloons are useful for **collecting** gases because they can expand as they fill up with more and more gas.

2 Making a gas

Get into groups. Your teacher will give you some baking soda, vinegar and a balloon.

a. Follow the instructions in your Workbook to make and collect a gas called carbon dioxide.

b. **Record** your observations.

WB 38

Extension

Over time the balloon will get smaller. What do you think has happened to the gas inside? How do you think this happened?

WB 39

Different gases have different properties. We can use the properties of a gas to identify it.

3 Testing a gas

Get into groups again.

a. Use a small candle in a jar to **test** the gas in your balloon.

b. Record what happens.

WB 39

A flame cannot burn in carbon dioxide. A fire extinguisher is a cylinder filled with a gas such as carbon dioxide.

Firefighters can use a carbon dioxide fire extinguisher to put out fires.

Yeast and carbon dioxide

Another way to make carbon dioxide is to use yeast. Carbon dioxide gas is made when yeast grows.

Yeast helps to make bread light and fluffy.

4 Making carbon dioxide with yeast

Work in pairs. Your teacher will give you some yeast and sugar.

a. Follow the instructions in your Workbook to set up an experiment as in the picture.

b. What happens when you leave the bottle in a warm place?

c. Test the gas in the same way as in Activity 3. How do you know that the gas is carbon dioxide?

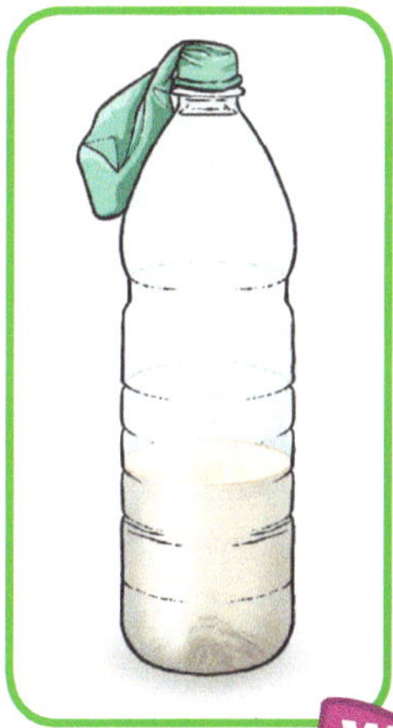

WB 40

Extension

Find out what increases the amount of carbon dioxide produced by yeast.

WB 40

What is a bubble?

Bubbles are like balloons made of a thin layer of liquid. A bubble is filled with gas, such as air.

5 Making bubbles

Get into groups.

a. Make some bubbles. You will need some washing-up liquid or liquid soap to begin.

b. Experiment with making bubbles.

- How can you make your bubbles big?
- How can you make bubbles that last for a long time?

WB 41

Interesting fact

The air around us is a mixture of gases. It contains mostly the gases nitrogen and oxygen. We cannot live without oxygen from the air.

Checklist

Complete these statements on page 41 of your Workbook.

- I can name some gases.
- I can describe two ways to make carbon dioxide.
- I can describe two properties of carbon dioxide.

2.5 Melting

In this section, I am learning:

- how solids change when they are heated
- how the particle model helps to explain these changes.

Key words

heat
melt
observe
temperature

Matin and Atiya are outside on a hot, sunny day. What is happening to their ice cream and chocolate?

What is melting?

When a solid turns into a liquid, we say the solid **melts**. Melting happens when we **heat** a solid.

We can use the particle model to explain how melting works:

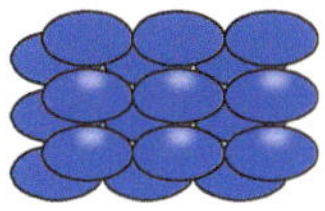

1 Heating a solid adds energy to the particles.

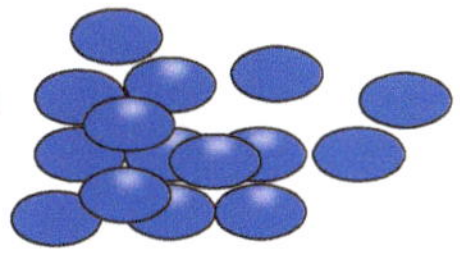

2 Eventually, the particles get so much energy that they are not held together anymore.

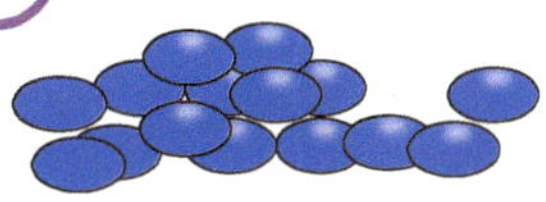

3 They start moving around, just like the particles in liquid do. The solid has now become a liquid.

Imagine particles in an ice cube. What happens to the shape of the solid as it melts? What is happening to the particles?

Ice is frozen water. It is a solid.

1 Investigating melting

Your teacher will give you a beaker of ice cubes and a bowl of warm water to investigate melting.

a. Observe the conditions at the start of your investigation.

b. Predict what will happen when you place the beaker of ice in the bowl of water.

c. Then place the beaker of ice in the bowl of water. Record your observations in your Workbook.

d. What did you find out? Write your conclusion in your Workbook.

WB 42–43

Extension

Where in your classroom do you think ice cubes will melt very fast? Give a reason for your answer.

WB 43

Do all solids melt in the same way?

Different solids have different properties. This means they may not behave in different ways when they are heated.

2 Exploring how different solids melt

Get into groups. Use warm water to find out how these solids melt.

butter wax chocolate

a. Describe how you will set up your investigation.

b. How long does it take for each solid to melt?

c. What do the results tell you about melting solids?

WB 44

Interesting fact

Not all solids melt at the same temperature. Some metals need to be heated to a very high temperature in a hot furnace before they will melt.

2.6 Freezing

In this section, I am learning:

- how liquids change when they are cooled
- to use the particle model to explain these changes.

Key words
cool
freeze, freezing

Look at the picture. What are the children making? How are they doing it?

What is freezing?

When a liquid **cools**, the particles lose energy. They move more slowly. If the liquid is cooled down enough, the particles will eventually stop moving altogether. This is how particles behave in a solid. The change from a liquid to a solid is called **freezing**.

Icicles are long icy spikes.

Interesting fact

One of the longest icicles ever seen hung from a bridge in Scotland. It was almost 9 m long.

Liquids take the shape of their container. When you **freeze** them, they will keep this shape. We can use moulds to make different-shaped solids when freezing liquids.

1 Freezing liquids

Your teacher will give you different liquids. Investigate whether they will freeze in the same time. You will freeze them inside containers of the same shape and size. This will make your investigation a fair test.

Record your results in your Workbook.

WB 45

We often use melting and freezing when we cook.

Solid chocolate melts when it is heated. It becomes a liquid.

Melted chocolate turns back into a solid when it is cooled.

2 Exploring melting and freezing

Make a chocolate fruit stick as explained in your Workbook.

How did the chocolate change?

WB 46

Freezing food is a way to keep the food fresh for a long time. We can warm up frozen food so it is ready to eat.

Extension

Research three other uses of melting and freezing in the home or in industry.

WB 46

Interesting fact

Petrol freezes at about −40 °C. So, even if it is snowing outside where you live, petrol will likely still be liquid.

Checklist

Complete these statements on page 46 of your Workbook.

- I can describe how to melt a solid.
- I can describe the changes to a solid as it melts.
- I know that freezing is the reverse of melting.
- I can describe the changes to a substance as it freezes.
- I can describe some uses of melting and freezing.

2.7 Heating liquids and cooling gases

In this section, I am learning:

- how liquids like water change when they are heated
- what happens when a gas is cooled.

Key words

boil
condense
evaporation
water vapour

Look at the picture. What is happening? In what state of matter is the water?

Heating liquids

When a liquid is heated, the particles gain energy. Eventually, the particles have enough energy to escape the liquid. They become particles in a gas. When a liquid changes to a gas, we call it **evaporation**.

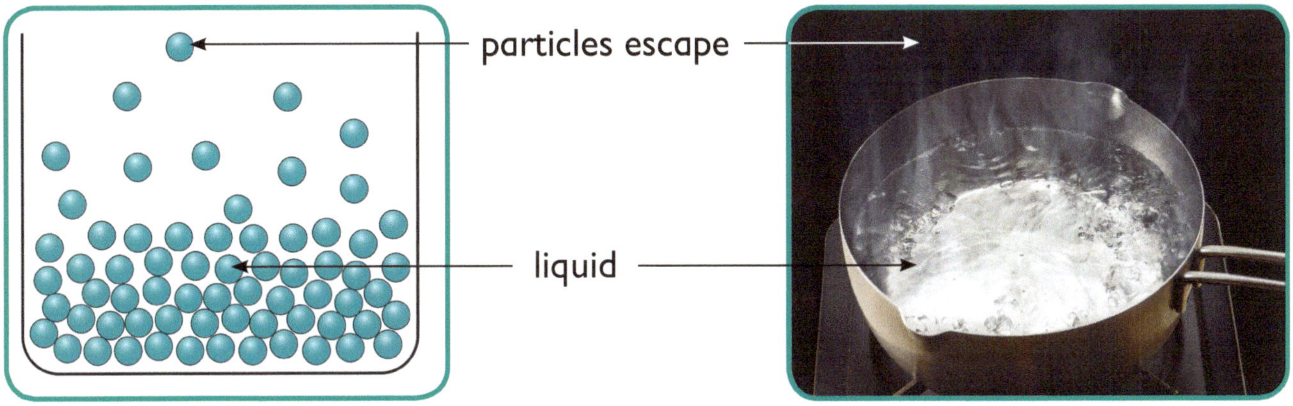

When a liquid is heated and we see many bubbles forming, we say the liquid **boils**. The bubbles are filled with gas. Water boils at 100 °C.

Cooling a gas

When gas particles meet a cold surface, they lose energy. They slow down and move closer together. The gas changes into the liquid state. We say the gas has **condensed** to become a liquid.

Water vapour condenses on the outside of a cold bottle.

1 What happens when you breathe on a mirror?

Breathe on a mirror.

a. What do you see?

b. Why do you think this happens?

WB 47

The air you breathe out contains some **water vapour**. This is water as a gas.

The mirror is colder than the space inside your lungs. When the water vapour makes contact with the cold mirror, the water vapour condenses. Tiny droplets of liquid water form.

2 Boiling and condensing water

Look at the diagrams in your Workbook that show water changing state.

Match each label with the correct diagram.

WB 48

✓ Checklist

Complete these statements on page 48 of your Workbook.

- I can describe what happens when a liquid boils.
- I know that cooling a gas will change it back to a liquid.
- I can recognise when a liquid is boiling and when a gas is cooling.

2.8 Changes of state

In this section, I am learning:

- how solids turn to liquids and liquids to gases
- that changes of state are reversible
- how to use a thermometer.

Key words
measure
reversible
thermometer

Changing state

You already know that the three states of matter are solid, liquid and gas. Matter can change from one state to another by heating or cooling.

Melting and freezing are examples of changes of state.

- During melting, the solid state changes to the liquid state.
- During freezing, the liquid state changes to the solid state.

Your teacher will show you a burning candle. What states of matter do you see?

Can you see the matter changing state? What gives you this idea?

Evaporation and condensation are also changes of state.

- When a liquid evaporates, it becomes a gas.
- When a gas condenses it becomes a liquid.

In the kitchen, steam will condense on a cold window.

Rocks are solid. If rocks become hot enough they can melt.

It is so hot deep inside the Earth that the rock melts. We can see this change of state when a volcano erupts.

1 Identifying changes of state

Watch a video clip of a volcano erupting.

a. What changes of state do you see?

b. In your Workbook, describe what happens when a volcano erupts.

WB 49

Melting and freezing are opposites. Solid becomes liquid. Liquid becomes solid.

Evaporation and condensing are opposites. Liquid becomes gas. Gas becomes liquid.

We say the changes caused by these processes are **reversible**.

2 Changing state and changing back

Work with your partner.

a. Plan an experiment to investigate water changing state.

b. Then carry out the experiment. Write about it in your Workbook.

WB 50

Using a thermometer correctly

A **thermometer** has a coloured liquid inside. A temperature scale is marked on the outside. The level of the coloured liquid shows the temperature.

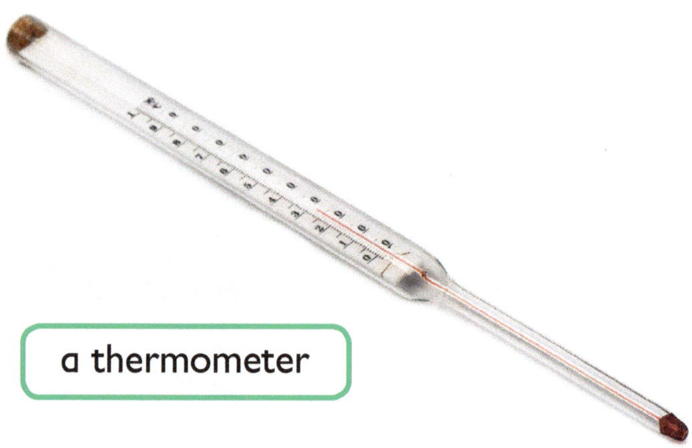

a thermometer

To use a thermometer correctly, hold it upright in the substance. The bulb should not touch the bottom of the container. If the bulb rests on the bottom of the container, the measurement will not be correct.

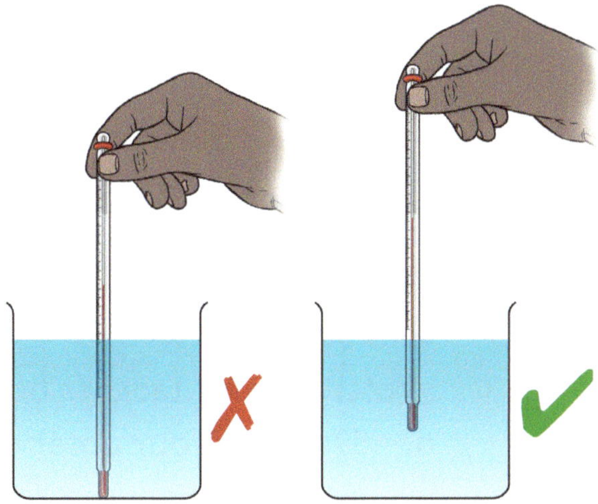

3 Reading a thermometer

Look at the pictures in your Workbook.

What temperature does each thermometer show?

WB 51

The melting point of a solid is the temperature at which it becomes a liquid.

4 At what temperature does ice melt?

Use a thermometer to **measure** the temperature as ice is heated.

WB 51

Extension

How might your results be different if you used a different amount of ice?

a. Do you think the melting temperature will be different?

b. Do you think the time it takes to change state might be different?

Give a reason for each answer.

WB 52

The boiling point of a liquid is the temperature at which it boils.

5 At what temperature does water boil?

We make tea with boiling water. We cook with boiling water.

Watch as your teacher boils some water.

a. Describe your observations.

b. At what temperature does water boil?

WB 52

Extension

a. Find out the boiling and melting temperatures of three different substances.

b. The boiling and melting point of a substance are never the same. Why do you think this is?

WB 52–53

Hint

Think about what is happening to the particles during melting and boiling.

Interesting fact

It is very dangerous to leave petrol out in the sun. The liquid particles soon escape as a gas. The gas can easily catch fire if there are any flames nearby.

Checklist

Complete these statements on page 53 of your Workbook.

- I can describe all the changes that occur when solids, liquids and gases are heated and cooled.
- I can use a thermometer correctly to measure temperature.
- I know the temperature at which ice melts.
- I know the temperature at which water boils.

What have I learnt?

Answer these questions on the worksheet your teacher gives you.

1. Which state of matter does each diagram represent?

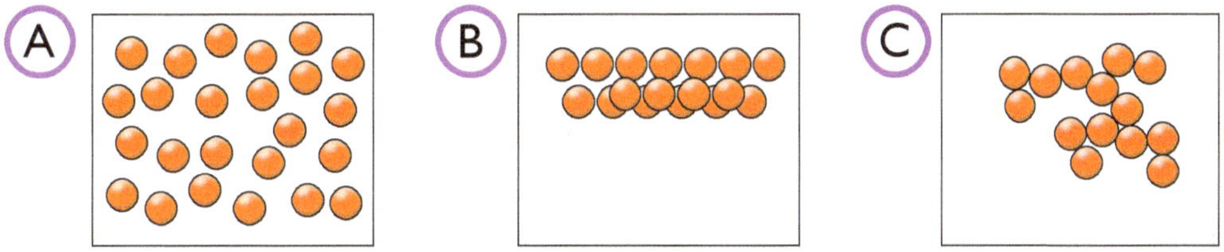

2. Hakim carries out an experiment to measure how fast a liquid flows. He has got the steps in a muddle. What order should the steps be in?

   A Start the timer.
   B Measure the time taken for 10 ml to flow into the cylinder.
   C Pour the liquid into the funnel.
   D Place the funnel in the measuring cylinder.
   E Get a funnel, a small measuring cylinder and a timer.

3. Choose words from the box to complete the sentences. Some words may be used more than once.

boils	freeze	gas	melts	liquid

When we heat ice, it ____ and turns into a ____.

When liquid water is heated to the point where bubbles form, it ____. The bubbles are filled with ____.

When gas cools, it turns back into a ____.

When we ____ the ____ water it becomes a solid.

4 What is the temperature shown on each thermometer?

a.

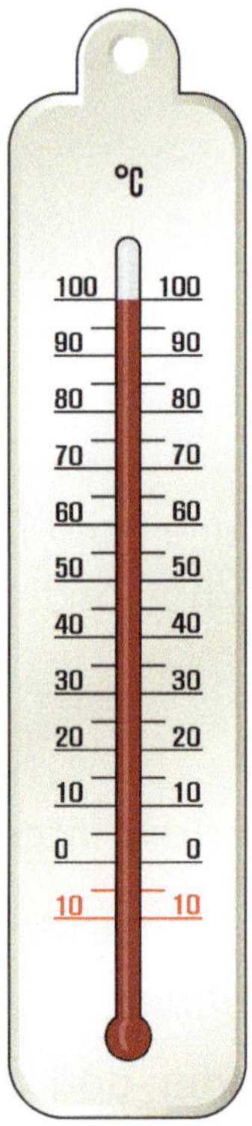

b.

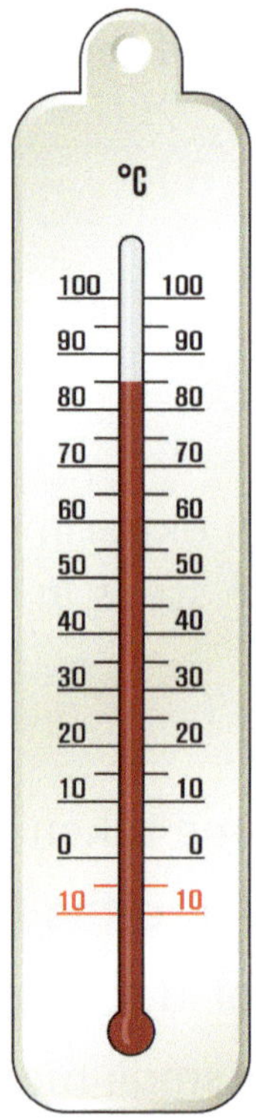

c.

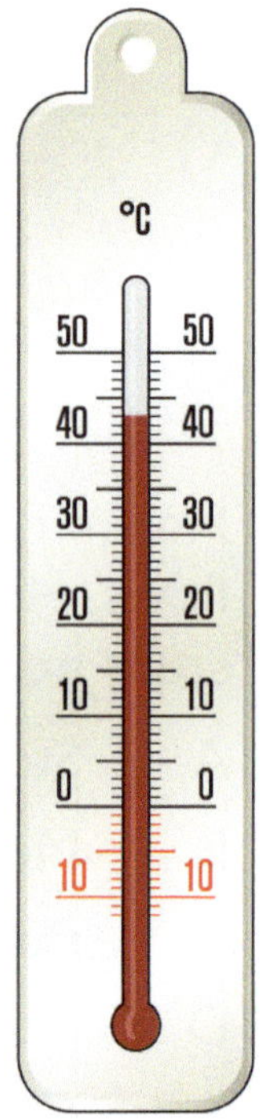

5 **a.** At what temperature does ice melt?

b. At what temperature does water boil?

3 How magnets work

Key words

attract
force
magnet
poles
repel

In this unit, I am learning:

- to identify magnetic metals
- about the poles of a magnet
- about attraction and repulsion
- how to use magnets correctly so that they keep their strength
- how we use magnets in everyday life and in industry.

What can you see in the picture? Do you know how it works?

3.1 Properties of magnets

In this section, I am learning:

- about magnetic metals
- about the poles of a magnet
- what happens when the poles of two magnets are brought together.

Key words

attract
copper
force
horseshoe magnet
magnet
north
repel
south
wand magnet
bar magnet
floating magnet
gold
iron
metal
poles
silver
steel

What do you already know about metals? Discuss your ideas with the class.

Magnetic metals

Most **metals** are solids. They are usually hard and shiny. Metals can conduct electricity and heat.

We can test for another property of metals using a **magnet**.

- If you hold a magnet over a metal object and it is pulled towards the magnet, the metal is magnetic.
- If the metal object is not pulled towards the magnet, the metal is non-magnetic.

Iron, **steel**, cobalt and nickel are magnetic metals.

iron

steel

gold

Copper, **gold** and **silver** are non-magnetic metals.

copper

What is a magnet?

A magnet is a piece of magnetic metal that can pull other magnetic metals towards it. A magnet has a magnetic **force**.

Magnets can have different shapes. They can be different sizes. Some have a casing so that we can handle them easily, like this **wand magnet**. We often use a **horseshoe magnet** or a bar magnet in Science class.

How can you find out if a piece of metal is a magnet or simply magnetic? Talk about your ideas with your partner.

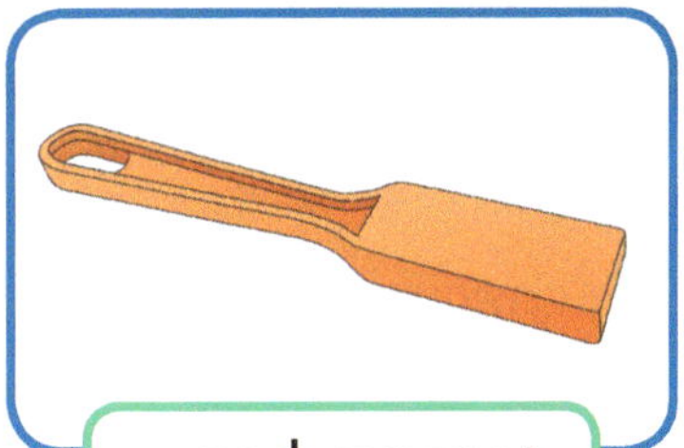

wand magnet

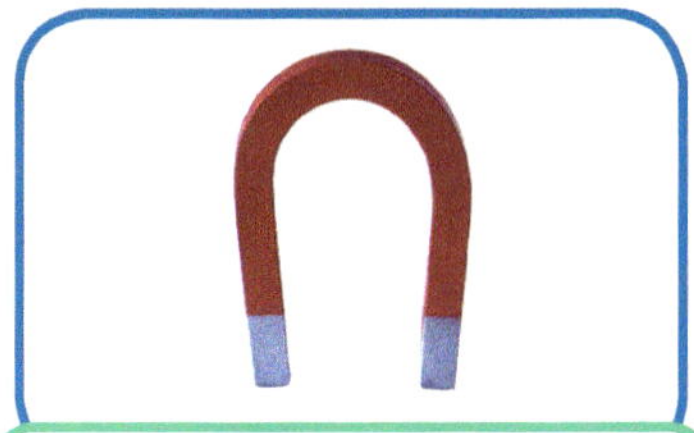

horseshoe magnet

Although magnets do not all look the same, they all work in the same way.

1 Exploring magnets

Get into groups. Your teacher will give you some magnets.

a. Can you say which magnet is which?

b. Test the magnets to see how they work.

c. Which objects in your classroom are magnetic?

WB 56

We call the two ends of a magnet **poles**.
The magnetic force is strongest at the poles.

If the poles of two magnets are brought towards each other, they can **attract** by pulling together, or **repel** by pushing apart.

2 Attraction and repulsion

Get into pairs. Your teacher will give you two **bar magnets**.

Let one magnet hang freely, like this.

Observe what happens when you bring the other magnet towards the hanging one.

a. When do the magnets attract each other?

b. When do the magnets repel each other?

WB 57

One end of a magnet is called the **north** pole. The opposite end is called the **south** pole. If you have two magnets, opposite poles will attract each other. Poles of the same type will repel each other.

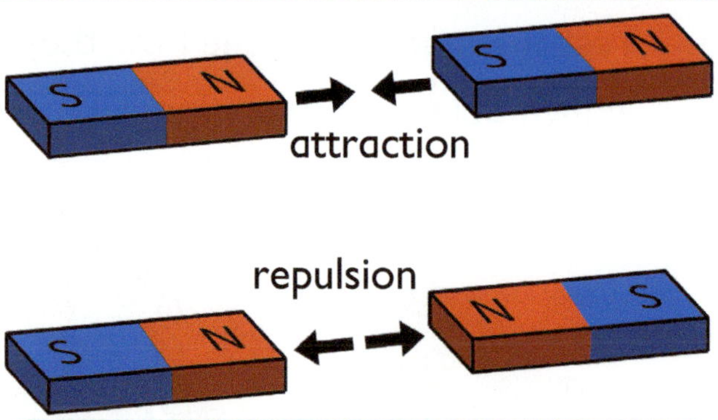

Attraction and repulsion are forces.

3 Comparing different magnets

Get into pairs. Your teacher will give you some magnets.

a. Choose two magnets that look the same. Bring them together in different ways.

b. Repeat this with two magnets that look different.

c. What can you conclude about magnets?

WB 57–58

Magnets can be different shapes or sizes, but they all have a north pole and a south pole. North and south poles are opposite poles.

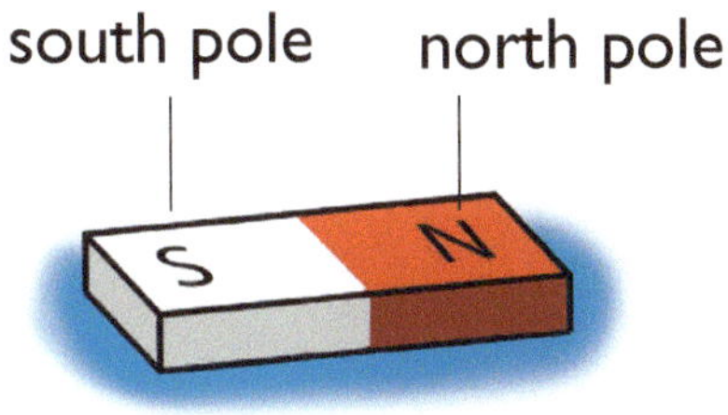

A bar magnet

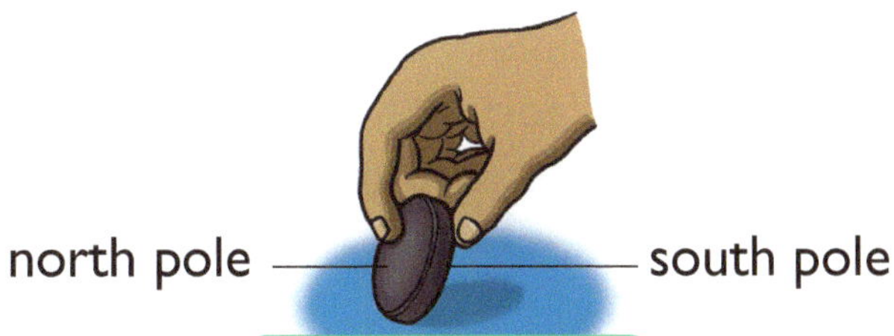

A disc magnet

4 Explaining how magnets work

Look at the picture. How do you think **floating magnets** work?

a. Identify the poles on each magnet.

b. Complete the sentences in your Workbook to explain how each diagram works.

WB 59

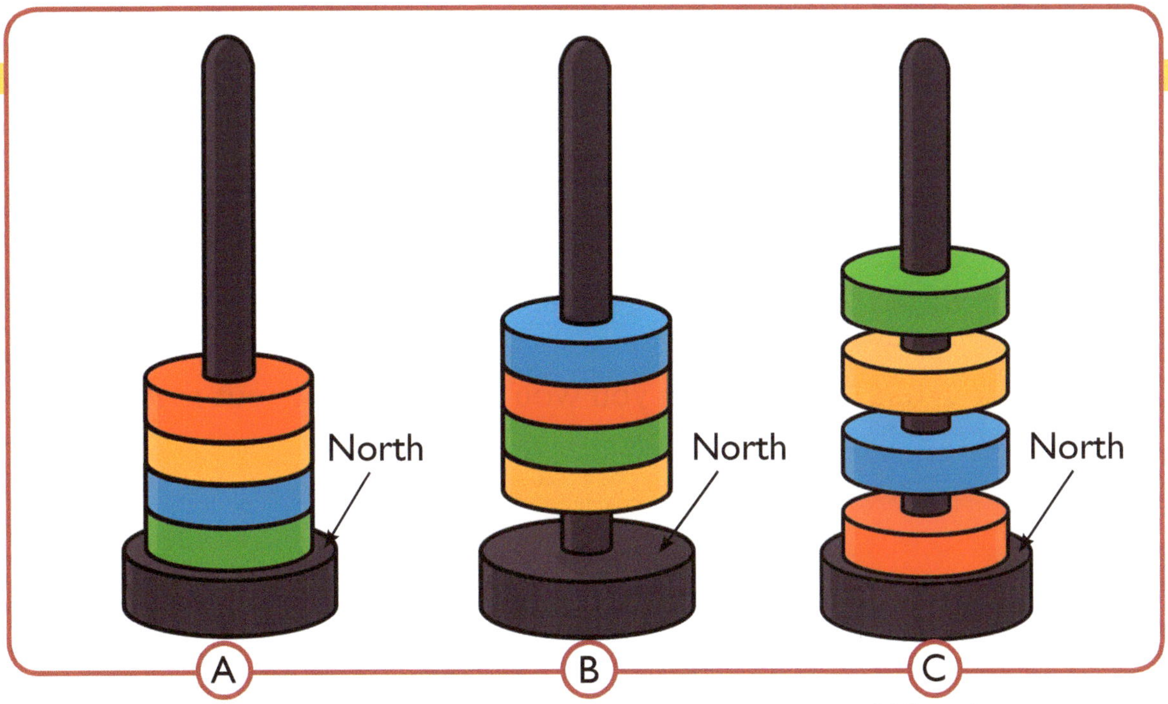

Why are all the magnets stuck together?

Why is the first magnet floating while all the others are stuck together?

Why do the top three magnets float?

Hint

The black stand base is magnetic. The top of the base is a north pole.

The discovery of magnets and understanding how magnets work have made many inventions possible. One example is a compass. You will learn more about how a compass works later.

A lodestone is a piece of rock that is a natural magnet.

Interesting fact

The Ancient Greeks discovered that a lodestone hanging freely always pointed in the same direction. Early Chinese sailors used lodestones to make the first compasses.

Extension

a. What have you learnt about magnets so far? Prepare a short talk to communicate your ideas.

b. Think of another question you would like to ask about magnets. Research the answer.

WB 60

Checklist

Complete these statements on page 60 of your Workbook.

- I can name four magnetic metals.
- I can recognise magnets of different shapes.
- I know that all magnets have a north pole and a south pole.
- I know that two poles of the same type repel each other.
- I know that opposite poles of two magnets attract each other.

3.2 How to use magnets

In this section, I am learning:

- how to use magnets correctly
- to test the strength of magnets.

Key words

apparatus
equipment
evidence
fair test
keepers
measure
plan
predict
reliable
repeat

If two magnets are the same size, can one magnet be stronger than the other?

Look at the picture to give you some ideas. Talk about it with your partner.

Magnets can have different strengths, even if they look the same. We can test the strength of a magnet in different ways. One way is to **measure** how close a magnet has to be to a steel paper clip before the paper clip starts to move.

1 Testing the strength of a magnet

Work with your group.

a. **Plan** a simple investigation to test the strength of a magnet. Look at the **apparatus** and **equipment** Xu and Tala have put together to give you some ideas.

- How will you make sure it is a **fair test**?
- What **evidence** will you look for?

Then carry out your investigation.

b. How strong is your magnet?

c. How do different magnets compare?

WB 61–62

Extension

Magnets can be used to hold different objects, such as tools and knives. Suggest how we can test the strength of these magnets.

WB 62

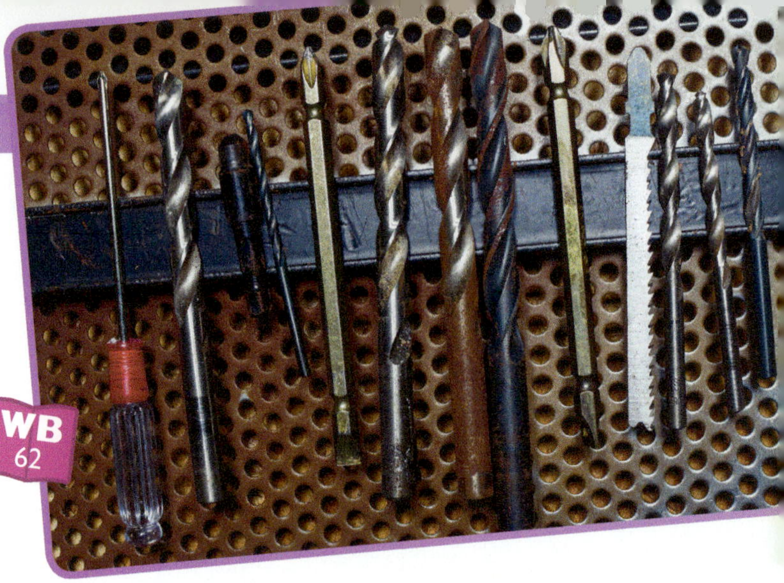

Can the strength of a magnet change?

Magnets can lose their strength if we do not use them correctly. To protect magnets and keep them strong we should:

- *never* drop them on the floor
- *never* bang them together
- *always* store them with **keepers**.

Your teacher will show you what a keeper looks like and how it should be used.

2 Strong and weak magnets

Your teacher will give you some identical magnets that have been handled differently.

a. Can you **predict** which magnet is strongest?

b. Test the magnets. Your test will be more **reliable** if you **repeat** it.

c. Use a chart to show your results. What did you find out?

WB 63

Interesting fact

The Earth's core is made of iron, which makes it act like a magnet. But it is not very strong. Scientists have discovered stars that are billions of times stronger magnets than the Earth. These stars are called magnetars.

3.3 Uses of magnets

In this section, I am learning:

- about the uses of magnets.

Key words
collect
compass
magnetic

Why are magnets useful in these three pictures? How do they work?

Talk about your ideas with your teacher.

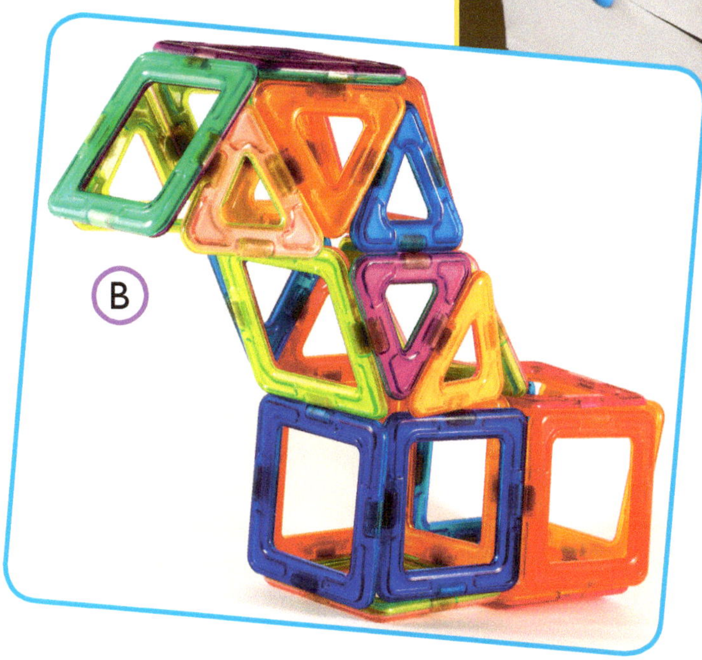

Magnets have many uses in our lives. They can be used to hold things together or keep things apart. They can even be used to store information, like on a bank card or a key card.

1 How magnets are used in our world

Your teacher will show you a video about how magnets are used.

a. Make some notes as you learn more about magnets.

b. Get into groups. Make a poster about how we use magnets in our lives.

WB 64

Using a compass

Remember that the centre of the Earth contains iron and is **magnetic**. Without this we could not find our way with a **compass**. The Earth acts like a big bar magnet with a north pole and a south pole.

The needle of a compass is a small magnet. It spins freely around a pin. The needle is attracted to one of the Earth's magnetic poles. The direction the needle points in is called north.

The magnet in a compass points towards the north.

Look at the picture. How does the compass help the children to reach their destination?

We can use magnets to help us solve problems.

2 Designing your own use for a magnet

Get into groups.

How can you use a magnet to solve one of the problems described in your Workbook? Show your ideas in your Workbook.

WB 65

Interesting fact

New magnetic materials are being developed. They are much stronger than normal magnets. They are used in wind turbines, MRI scanners, brakes on cars, and even in space projects to **collect** magnetic dust from Mars.

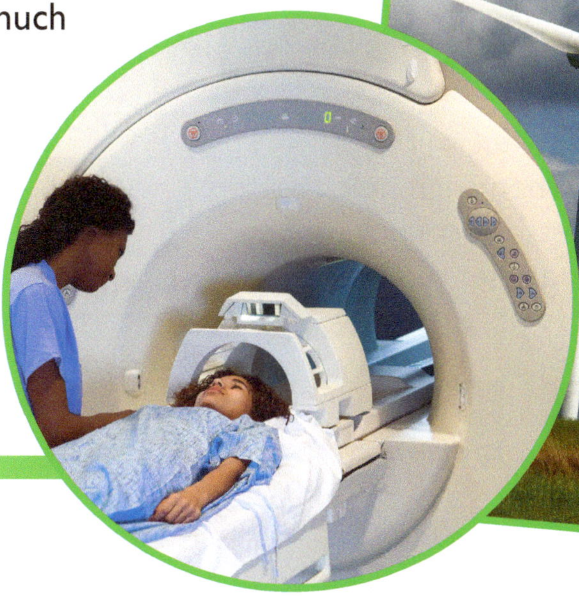

Extension

Imagine a world without magnets. Write a short description of all the things we would not have. How would this affect our lives?

WB 66

Checklist

Complete these statements on page 66 of your Workbook.

- I know how to handle magnets correctly.
- I can describe how to test the strength of a magnet.
- I can name some uses of magnets in our lives.

What have I learnt?

Answer these questions on the worksheet your teacher gives you.

1. Ari and Jake are testing materials. What will happen?

2. Describe what will happen when each pair of magnets is brought closer together.

3. Which one of these statements is true?
   - **a.** Magnets always attract each other.
   - **b.** If like poles of two magnets face each other, the magnets will repel.
   - **c.** Magnets always point towards a compass.

4. Bahir bought two new magnets. He tested them on many different materials on the way home. He dropped them several times and banged them against each other all the time. When Bahir got home, he tested his magnets again. What do you think happened?

5. List five different uses for magnets.

4 Habitats

In this unit, I am learning:

- about different local habitats and how to investigate them
- about the animals and plants that live in different global habitats
- how to use an identification key
- how human activity affects the environment
- about environmental disasters and how we respond
- how to care for the environment at school.

Key words
development
disaster
environment
habitat
key
pollution

What habitats can you see in the picture?

4.1 Local habitats

In this section, I am learning:

- to describe different local habitats
- to investigate the animals and plants found in local habitats.

Key words

animals, apparatus, brick wall, collect, creatures, environment, equipment, habitat, local, log pile, meadow, measurements, plan, plants, pond, pooter, repeat, results, stones

The space around us is called the **environment**. The environment includes living and non-living things. Living things in our environment include **plants**, **animals** and other organisms. Soil, water, air, buildings and roads are non-living things in our environment.

Humans are part of the environment. Our environment affects how we live. If our environment changes, then how we live changes too.

Habitats

Where you live is your **habitat**. Your habitat is part of your **local** environment. A habitat provides living things with food, shelter, water and space to live and breed.

Look at the pictures. Are they both habitats? Why do you say so?

Talk about your ideas in a group.

A habitat can be as small as a log pile or a pile of stones. Or it can be big, like a garden or even a rainforest.

A habitat has to provide the right conditions for the organisms that live there.

A brick wall like this is a suitable habitat for small plants.

Investigating habitats

We can investigate local habitats to learn more about our environment. When we investigate a habitat, we often have to collect plants or animals.

Animals and plants are living things. We must respect them and treat them carefully during our investigations. Also remember that it can be dangerous to handle some animals or plants. We must work responsibly so that we stay safe when investigating a habitat.

A pond gives fish and water plants everything they need to survive.

1 Rules for investigating a habitat

Get into groups. Think about working responsibly when investigating a habitat.

a. What should you do to treat plants and animals respectfully?

b. How can you keep safe during your investigation?

Write your ideas in your Workbook.

Then share your ideas with the rest of the class to make a class list.

WB 68

How to investigate plants and animals in a habitat

We can use different types of **equipment** to investigate plants and animals in a habitat.

- Nets are useful for collecting butterflies, moths or fish.
- We can collect small **creatures** living on the ground using a pitfall trap.
- A magnifying glass helps us to look at features of plants or animals closely.
- A **pooter** is useful for collecting small invertebrates.

Using a pooter

What other types of equipment or apparatus can you use to learn about a habitat?

It is easy to make your own pooter for your investigations.

2 Making a pooter

Get into pairs. Your teacher will give you some materials.

a. Follow the instructions in your Workbook to make a pooter.

b. Practise using your pooter. **Repeat** it a few times.

How does the pooter work?

WB 69

Extension

What are the advantages of using a pooter?

Why does the end of the straw you suck through have some cloth over it?

WB 70

We need a plan before we go out to investigate a habitat. If we plan ahead we will know what equipment to take and what steps we have to follow.

3 Planning to investigate habitats

Get into pairs.

Look at the meadow in this picture.

Imagine you are planning to investigate this habitat. Write some notes in your Workbook.

- **a.** What is this habitat like?
- **b.** What type of animals and plants do you think you will find?
- **c.** What do you want to find out about this habitat?
- **d.** What equipment will you need for your investigation?
- **e.** What measurements will you take?
- **f.** What safety measures will you need to think about?

WB 70–71

Now that you have some ideas about how to plan a habitat investigation, you can prepare to investigate a habitat in your local area.

Using the right equipment helps us to investigate a habitat successfully.

4 Investigating habitats

Get into groups.

Look at the habitats your teacher shows you as you walk around your school grounds.

- **a.** Choose one of the habitats to investigate.
- **b.** Plan how you will investigate this habitat.
- **c.** Carry out your investigation. What did you find out? Record your observations in your Workbook.

WB 72–73

Reflect on your findings

It is a good idea to share the findings from our investigations with other people. This can help us to understand the **results** better, give us ideas for further investigations or help us improve our plans. In this way we can learn more about the world around us.

Scientists share their findings by writing about them, presenting a talk or making a poster.

5 Making a model habitat

Get into your groups as for Activity 4. Your teacher will give you some materials.

a. Use them to make a model of the habitat you investigated.

b. Use your model to tell the rest of your class about your findings.

WB 74

What do you think Naomi can tell others about this habitat? Discuss your ideas with your partner.

Extension

Think back to one of the habitats you investigated. Think about how it provides food, water, shelter and space for animals and plants to live and breed. Write a paragraph in your Workbook about this habitat.

WB 74

Interesting fact

Tiny creatures like these live in pond water. They are so small that there can be many of them in a single drop of water. We can use a microscope to observe them closely.

4.2 World habitats

In this section, I am learning:

- about different world habitats
- how different animals are suited to their environment.

Key words

bar chart
leaf pile
predict
research
table
woodland

There are different habitats in the world. The animals that live in each one are suited to the conditions there.

Look at the picture of a coral reef. Where will you find this habitat?

What kind of things live there? How are they suited to the habitat?

Talk about your ideas with your teacher.

Animals such as penguins, whales and seals live in the cold Antarctic. They are suited to live in icy cold conditions.

The living things in a habitat need each other. Some animals eat the plants in a habitat. They are called herbivores. Other animals eat the herbivores. This is called a food chain.

Herbivores such as giraffe live in the African savannah.

1 Researching a habitat

Look at the photos of habitats you have seen so far. Here are some more.

Choose one of the habitats you have seen so far. Do some **research** about it.

a. What is the habitat like?

b. Which plants and animals live there?

c. How are the plants and animals suited to the conditions in the habitat?

WB 75–76

rainforest

desert

freshwater lake

Every part of the food chain needs to be healthy for animals to survive in a habitat. For example, the caterpillars of some butterflies can eat only certain kinds of plant. If their habitat does not have the right plant, they will not survive.

2 Matching animals and plants in a habitat

Look at the pictures of plants and animals in your Workbook.

a. Which pairs belong together?

b. In which habitat will you find each pair?

WB 77

Imagine you are a plant or an animal. Which habitat would you be best suited to? Talk about it with your partner.

Where the conditions are right, many animals of the same type may decide to live there.

Woodlice are harmless invertebrates. You may find them under a **leaf pile**, logs or other plant material. Sometimes they live in houses too.

woodlice

3 Investigating the best conditions for woodlice

Get into groups.

a. **Predict** which condition will suit woodlice best.

b. Use a choice chamber to investigate. Record your results in the **table** in your Workbook.

c. Draw a **bar chart** to show your results.

d. Was your prediction correct?

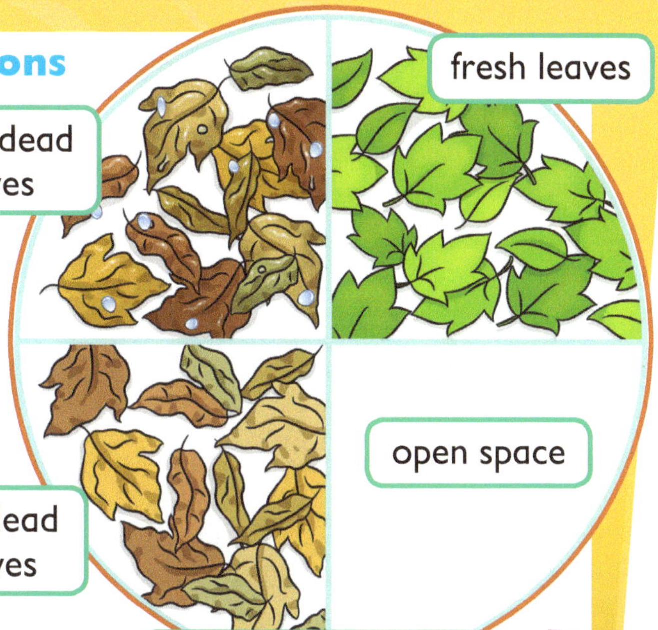

a choice chamber

WB 78

Extension

Look at this **woodland** habitat.

a. Imagine a new animal that would be at home here.

b. Think of a name for your new animal.

c. What makes this animal suited to this habitat?

WB 79

Hint

Think about what the animal would eat and how it would move. What are the conditions like in this habitat?

Each animal needs its own living space, so that it feels comfortable. It needs enough space to live and enough space to find all the food it needs. This space is called its territory.

You can see animals from many different habitats across the world in a zoo. When animals live in a zoo, their territories are smaller than when they are in the wild. Zookeepers have to think carefully about how much space each animal needs to live well.

Imagine that you work in a zoo. How would you design a space that is right for a buffalo? What about a space for a polar bear?

Talk about your ideas with your partner.

Interesting fact

The oceans cover the biggest part of the Earth. Scientists estimate that more than half of all life on Earth is found in the oceans. We have explored less than a tenth of this space.

The oceans are home to many different plants and animals.

Checklist

Complete these statements on page 80 of your Workbook.

- I can describe what a habitat is.
- I know how to investigate a habitat responsibly.
- I can name different local and world habitats.
- I can name some animals and plants that live in a specific habitat.
- I know that plants and animals are suited to their habitats.

4.3 Identifying animals and plants

In this section, I am learning:

- to describe the characteristics of animals and plants
- how an identification key works
- to identify plants or animals using an identification key.

Key words
features
identification key
identify
questions

Sometimes we come across an unfamiliar plant or animal. To help us **identify** an unfamiliar organism, we can look at its **features**. We can try to group the organism with others of a similar kind that are already familiar to us.

Imagine you have a friend who has never seen a bird or a bee. He knows that they both have wings. How would you help your friend to identify a bee and a bird?

When scientists have to identify an unfamiliar organism, they ask questions about its features.

1 Describing animals

Carl and Lara each visited a new place during their holiday. They each sent a photograph of an interesting animal they saw.

You do not know which picture came from Carl and which one was from Lara. How can you find out?

Work with your partner.

a. Write down the features of each animal in your Workbook.

b. Turn these features into **questions** that can be answered by saying "yes" or "no".

c. Now ask your partner to pretend they are Carl or Lara. Ask them your questions. Which animal did they see?

WB 81

Animal 1

Animal 2

Some features can be the same in different animals. To tell these animals apart we have to look for features that are different.

2 What am I?

Get into pairs. Take it in turns to play the "What am I?" game.

a. Let your partner choose one of the cards your teacher gives you.

b. Now ask your partner questions to find out what animal is shown on the card.

c. How many questions does it take to get the answer?

WB 82

Identification keys

An **identification key** is useful to identify an unfamiliar plant or animal. It is made up of questions about the plant or animal's features, like in the "What am I?" game.

A successful identification key includes questions that will help you tell the plant or animal apart from other similar ones.

Look at these three animals.

In an identification key, would it be useful to ask if they are black?

What other questions could you ask?

Here is an example of an identification key.

Answer each question in the key with "yes" or "no". This lets you sort the animals into one of two groups each time.

Follow the arrows to another question or the name of the animal.

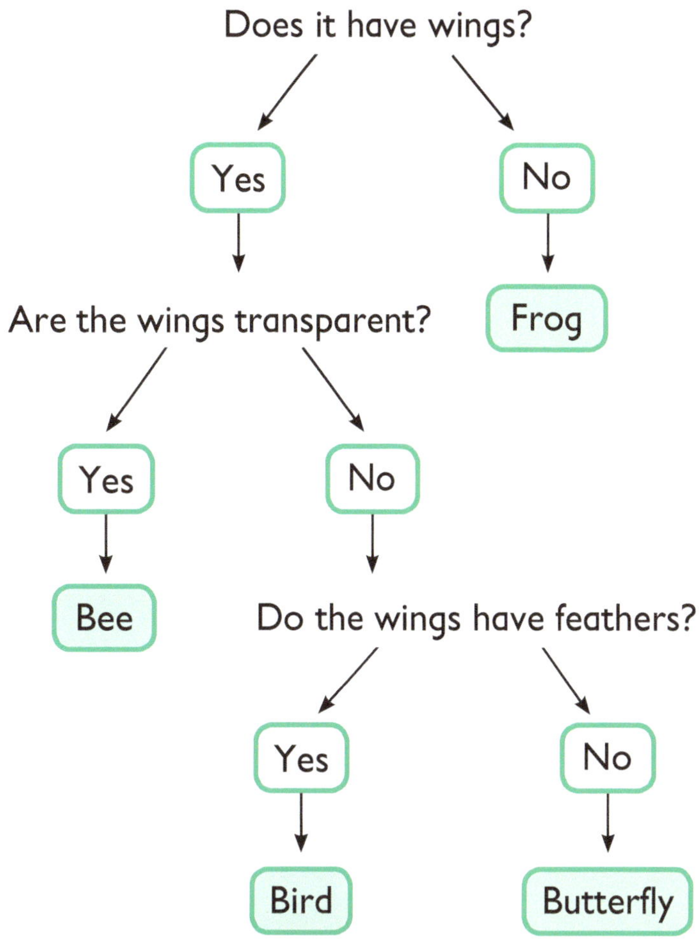

Which animal is shown in each picture? Tell your teacher.

Now that you know how an identification key works, you can make your own.

3 Working with a simple identification key

Look at the pictures.

a. Which features can describe each animal?

b. Use your observations to complete the identification key in your Workbook.

WB 82–83

An identification key can help us to find the names of plants.

4 An identification key for plants

Which trees are shown in the pictures?

a. Look at the leaves of different trees in your Workbook. Complete the identification key.

b. Then use the key to identify the trees shown here.

WB 84

Good observation skills will help you to learn more about the plants and animals in your local environment.

Extension

Jayesh wants to identify these snakes. He made some observations.

Use his questions in your Workbook to make an identification key.

Then use the key to identify the snake in each picture.

WB 85

A

B

C

D

✓ Checklist

Complete these statements on page 86 of your Workbook.

- I can describe the features of plants and animals.
- I know how a simple identification key works.
- I can use my observations to make and use a simple identification key.

4.4 How human activity affects the environment

In this section, I am learning:

- how human activities can change local habitats
- that human activity can affect the environment negatively
- how science can help to solve these problems.

Key words
development
litter
pollution

Many people live in cities or towns. Many cities and towns have parks. A park is usually a large open space with lots of plants. It is a habitat for animals and plants. People also use the space for relaxing, enjoying nature and exercise.

But a city also needs enough houses and shops for all the people who live there. Sometimes large open spaces are used for new building **developments** rather than parks.

Do you think the new shopping centre in Tara's and Gavin's town is a good idea? Talk about your views with your group.

Planning can help

We know that animals and plants need certain conditions in their habitat. If the conditions are changed, the habitat can be affected in a negative way. So it is important to plan new developments carefully.

1 Researching local developments

Get into groups.

a. Research a new development in your neighbourhood, town or village.

b. How are local habitats affected?

c. What are the advantages and disadvantages of the development?

WB 87

A town's planning officer has to make sure that a new development does not affect the environment in a bad way. Planning officers need to know the local community's views before a project starts. By sharing our views and taking part in the process, we can work with the developers to care for the plants and animals around us.

2 Making our voice heard

Tara wrote a letter to her town's planning officer about a shopping centre that is being planned.

Get into pairs.

a. Read the letter in your Workbook.

b. Answer the questions that follow.

WB 88–89

Change and progress are always happening. It is important that developers, the community and scientists work together to protect our environment.

Extension

How can scientists work with developers and town planners to make sure that animals, plants and humans can live together?

WB 89

Interesting fact

In many countries, a development cannot take place if a rare or protected animal is found at the site. An example in the United Kingdom is the great crested newt.

Helping to solve a problem

In places where many people live together, litter can become a problem. Plastic waste especially is a problem. Many of the plastic items people throw away end up in rivers. The plastic eventually reaches the sea.

How do you think plastic litter affects ocean life? Talk about your views in your group.

3 Combatting plastic pollution

Your teacher will tell you about some innovative ideas to clean up plastic pollution.

Do some research with a partner to find out what else people are doing to help prevent or solve this problem.

Show your findings in your Workbook.

WB 90

Extension

Imagine you have been asked to design something to collect plastic from the ocean.

a. Write some notes about how your idea works in your Workbook.

b. Then draw and label your design.

WB 91

We can all be part of a solution.

4.5 Environmental challenges for the Earth

In this section, I am learning:

- about the difference between a natural disaster and a human-made disaster
- about environmental challenges and their causes.

Key words
disasters
earthquake
natural disaster
oil slick
predict
tsunami
volcano

You already know that human activity can affect local habitats. But the world sometimes faces environmental challenges on a much larger scale. Events that negatively affect animals, plants and humans over a large area are called environmental **disasters**.

Some of disasters are caused by natural events. Others are caused by human activity.

The photo shows a person clearing oil from the sea. What do you think has happened? Is this a natural or a human-made disaster?

Natural disasters

Millions of people are affected by **natural disasters** every year. **Earthquakes**, floods, hurricanes, **tsunamis** and volcanic eruptions are examples of natural disasters.

Many people are killed or injured during a natural disaster. It can destroy roads, bridges and buildings. It can cause power failures and disrupt water supplies. During a natural disaster, telephone lines and internet connections are often disrupted. This hinders communication with the outside world.

A powerful earthquake struck Haiti in 2010. About 250 000 people died and about 300 000 were injured.

1 Impact of natural disasters

Your teacher will show you some video clips about the effects of natural disasters.

How are local communities and habitats affected?

WB 92

Human-made disasters

Some environmental disasters are caused by human activity. Examples are wildfires that are caused by people working irresponsibly with open fires, or pollution such as an oil spill at sea. An **oil slick** can kill sea life and pollute beaches for a long time.

2 Impact of human-made disasters

Your teacher will show you a video about a human-made disaster.

a. How does the event affect people's lives?

b. How does the event affect the environment?

c. What can people do to manage the environmental effects of this disaster?

d. How can a similar disaster be prevented in future?

People can help to clean sea birds affected by an oil spill.

WB 93

Imagine there has been a hurricane where you live.

How would you be affected? How would you respond? How would you plan for the future? Discuss your ideas with your class.

A hurricane is a very powerful storm that develops over tropical oceans. It brings very strong winds and heavy rain, and can cause lots of damage if it reaches the land.

Many homes and buildings along the east coast of the United States were destroyed during Hurricane Sandy in 2012.

3 Hurricane Sandy

a. Read the case study about Hurricane Sandy in your Workbook.

b. Answer the questions that follow.

WB 94–95

Scientists such as meteorologists and geologists collect data to **predict** natural disasters. This gives us early warning and helps us to respond better.

In 2018, geologists used data to warn people that Mount Kilauea, an active **volcano** in Hawaii, was going to erupt. People were able to leave their homes in time and emergency workers could help to keep people and animals safe.

Extension

Research one of these natural disasters:

- The earthquake in Lombok Island, Indonesia in 2018
- The tsunami in Thailand in December 2004
- The volcanic eruption in Hawaii in 2018

Show what you find out in your Workbook.

WB 95

Interesting fact

In March 2010, a massive earthquake struck off the coast of Japan. It triggered a big tsunami. Although almost 45 000 buildings were destroyed, early warning systems allowed many people to escape in time.

4.6 Promoting environmental awareness

In this section, I am learning:

- to identify areas around my school that can be improved
- how to increase environmental awareness at school.

Key words

evidence
measure
recycle
test

Improving the environment

We have to care for the environment around us. It starts with doing small things, such as picking up litter or closing taps properly. Being aware of the environment around us will help us to see what we can do to care for it.

Look at the school in the picture. How can the environment be improved? Talk about some ideas with your partner.

If everyone does one small thing, it can have a big effect.

Monitoring an environment

If we monitor an environment, we can learn how to help it.

Environmental scientists monitor the environment. They can **test** the water in rivers for pollution. They can **measure** and record levels of pollution and tell people how to reduce it.

We all want to be proud of the environment around us. To help us improve the environment around us, we have to know if there are any problem areas. This means we have to collect some data and make observations.

Testing water quality helps us to protect rivers and streams around us.

Regular records of air quality can help to keep the air around us clean.

1 Monitoring your school environment

Get into groups.

a. Choose one of these focus areas.
   - How do you use energy at school?
   - Do you **recycle** at school?
   - How do you deal with litter at school?
   - How do you support wildlife in the habitats around your school?

b. Do research and collect some **evidence**.

c. Record your findings in the worksheet your teacher gives you.

WB 96

Recycling is good for the environment.

There are many things you can do to help the environment.

- You can turn off lights to save energy.
- You can collect litter around your school or in the area where you live.
- You can recycle paper, glass, waste food and other materials.

Extension

Use your observations from Activity 1 to prepare a presentation for your school assembly.

a. Outline all the things your school is doing well.

b. Suggest what you could do to improve the environment around your school.

c. Talk about how you can monitor thechanges.

Putting rubbish in a bin helps to keep our environment clean.

WB 96

Interesting fact

Glass can be recycled over and over. Recycling glass means we use less energy and raw materials to make new glass bottles or jars. This helps to protect our environment.

Checklist

Complete these statements on page 97 of your Workbook.

- I can describe the impact of local developments on habitats.
- I can name some natural disasters and some caused by humans.
- I understand the effects of environmental disasters.
- I can describe how we can respond to environmental disasters.
- I can help to care for the environment at school.

What have I learnt?

Answer these questions on the worksheet your teacher gives you.

1. Name three animals or plants you will find in each habitat:

   a. Desert **b.** Ocean **c.** Polar ice

2. Claudia investigated habitats for woodlice with a choice chamber. Here are her results.

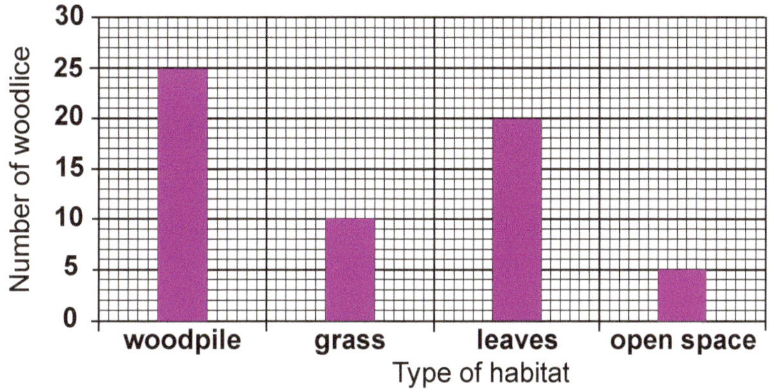

   a. In which habitat did she find the most woodlice?

   b. In which habitat did she find the fewest woodlice?

   c. What do the results tell you about the conditions woodlice prefer?

3. Describe three things you can do to help care for your environment.

4. Give two reasons why it is important not to pollute rivers.

5. Complete the sentences. Choose words from the box.

natural	ocean	environment	clean up	pollute
break down	oil slick	sea birds	human-made	

An oil spill is a ____ disaster. It harms ____ habitats. An ____ that washes up on a beach can ____ the environment for a long time. It takes a long time to ____ an oil spill. People can help to clean oil from fish and ____ to keep them safe.

5 Making circuits

In this unit, I am learning:

- how to make different electric circuits
- what happens when I add more components to a circuit
- about the job of a switch and how to use it in a circuit
- how a model can help us to understand how an electric circuit works
- that electricity can be dangerous and how to use it safely.

Key words
circuit
electricity
model
safety
switch

Look at the photo. How does the lamp work?

Does the lamp always shine?

5.1 Making circuits

In this section, I am learning:

- to construct different circuits
- what happens when I add more components to a circuit.

Key words

battery
buzzer
cell
circuit
compare
components
connector
construct
crocodile clip
current
electricity
lamp
lamp holder
motor
observe
wire
working circuit

Think back to your earlier work on **electricity**. You learnt how to put a **circuit** together.

What can you say about the circuits Shaan and Nadine are making?

A circuit is made up of different **components**, like these ones.

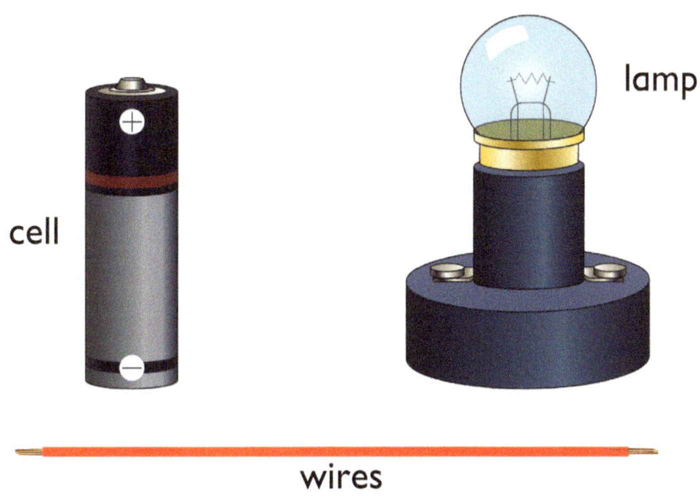

1 Making a circuit

a. Construct a working circuit. Remember to put the lamp in a lamp holder.

b. Does the lamp light up? Can you explain why?

WB 100

A lamp and a switch are components. There are different ways to connect a wire to a component, for example:

- using a plug that locates in a hole
- using a crocodile clip as a connector
- touching bare wires together.

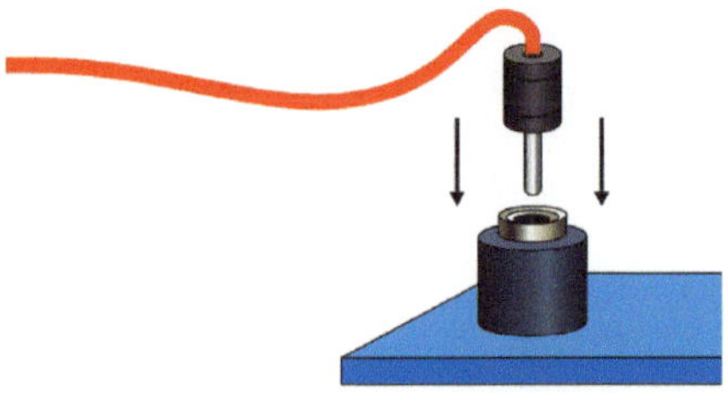

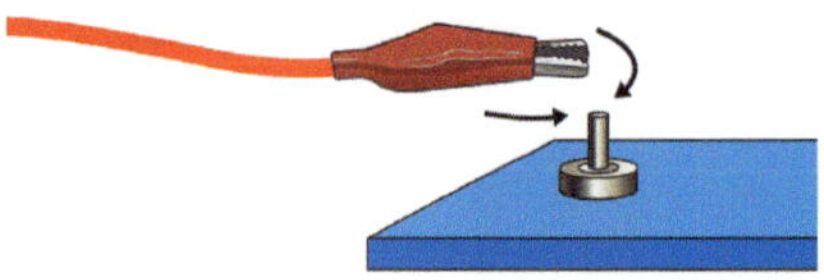

Whichever connection you use, it is important to make sure that the metal parts touch each other. This completes the electric circuit. When electricity moves around a circuit, this is called an electric current.

To make the components in a circuit work, a circuit needs a source of energy. A **cell** or a **battery** can be used as an energy source in a circuit.

Many people use the words "cell" and "battery" to mean the same thing. But in science, we use the word "battery" to describe a group of cells connected together. We should try to use the correct words: "cell" for a single cell and "battery" for many cells.

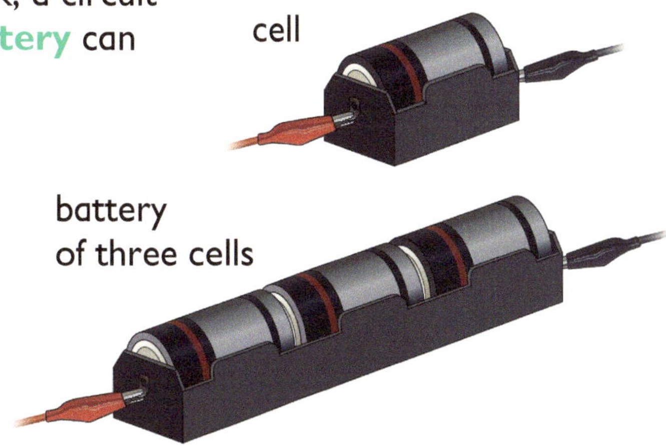

2 How does adding cells affect a circuit?

a. Construct these circuits. Use the components your teacher gives you.

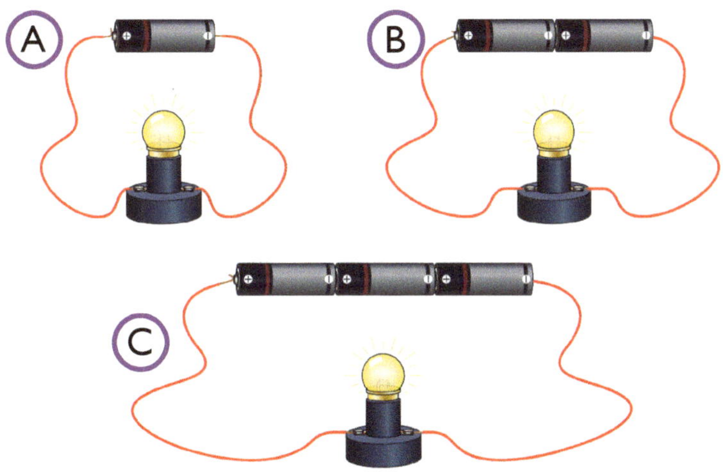

b. What happens when you add more cells to the circuit?

c. What have you discovered?

WB 100

Extension

Batteries come in all shapes and sizes. Why do you think this is useful?

WB 101

3 How does adding lamps affect a circuit?

a. Connect the circuits shown in the diagrams.

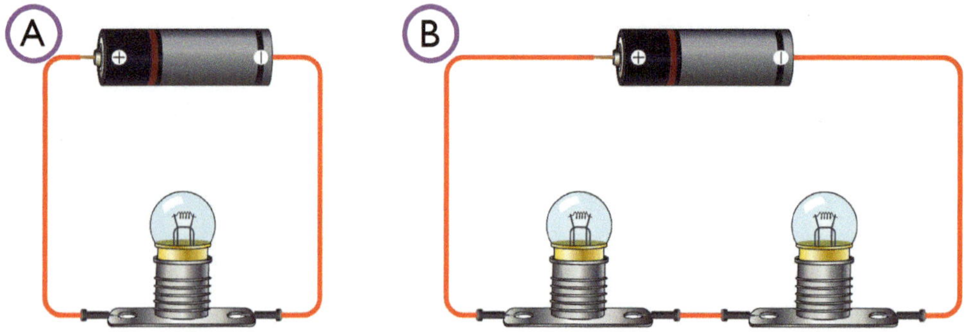

b. What do you **observe**?

c. What do you predict will happen if you add a third lamp?

WB 101

4 Making predictions

Look at the circuits in your Workbook.

a. Predict how the brightness of the lamps will **compare** between the three circuits.

b. Construct the circuits to test your prediction.

WB 102

We can also add a **motor** or a **buzzer** as components in a circuit.

5 Components of circuits

a. Connect a motor in a circuit. What do you observe?

b. Connect a buzzer in a circuit. What do you observe?

WB 103

Extension

a. What components can you see in the picture?

b. What will happen when the circuit is completed?

WB 104

Circuits make many things around us work, from a mobile phone to the lights in our homes.

Interesting fact

The first shopping street to be lit by electric lights was Electric Avenue in Brixton, London in 1888.

Checklist

Complete these statements on page 104 of your Workbook.

- I can name some circuit components.
- I know how to construct a circuit.
- I understand what happens when more cells and components are added to a circuit.

5.2 Switches

In this section, I am learning:

- what happens when there is a break in a circuit
- about the job of a switch
- how to make a switch.

Key words

break, complete, design, draw, make, plan, predict, switch, test

A flashing light can be used to send a message. How can Mr Tomkins make the light flash?

Why do we use flashing lights to send a message?

For a circuit to work, it has to be **complete**. This means that all the components must be connected together. There should not be a **break** in the circuit.

But sometimes it is useful to be able to break a circuit. We can use a **switch** to break a circuit.

When is it useful to have a break in a circuit? Share your ideas with your partner.

1 Comparing circuits

Look at the circuits in the diagrams.

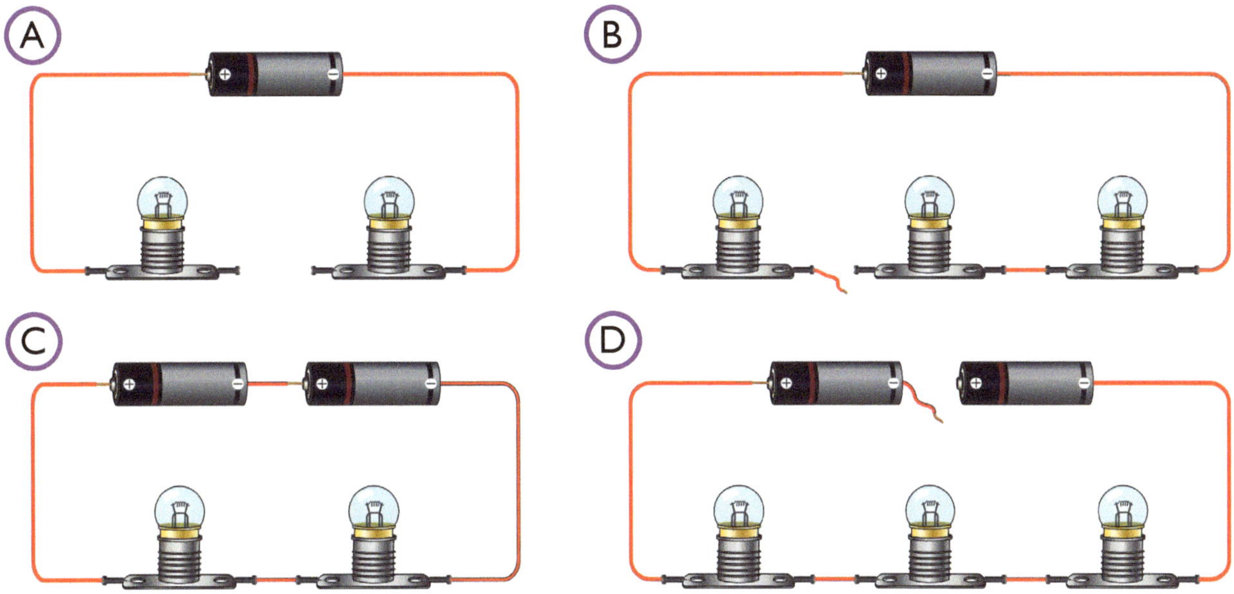

a. Predict whether these circuits will work.

b. Now make each circuit to test your predictions.

c. What is your conclusion?

WB 105

Switches

The purpose of a switch is to turn an electric circuit on or off.

When you set a switch to the "off" position, it breaks the circuit. The circuit is no longer complete.

If you set the switch to the "on" position, the circuit will be complete. The electricity can make the component work again.

2 Explaining how a flashlight works

Get into pairs. Look at the design of a simple flashlight.

Explain how the flashlight works.

WB 106

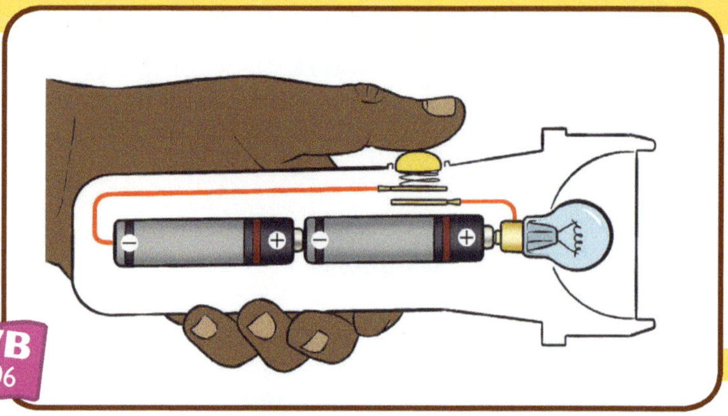

A switch can work with a pull cord or a button.

Extension

Go on a tour of your school.

a. How many different items can you find with a switch?

b. Draw a picture of some of the items. Show how the switches look.

⚠ Do not touch any electrical items on your tour, as they may be hot.

WB 106

3 Making your own switch

Get into groups.

Look at the circuit. It uses a switch made from simple materials.

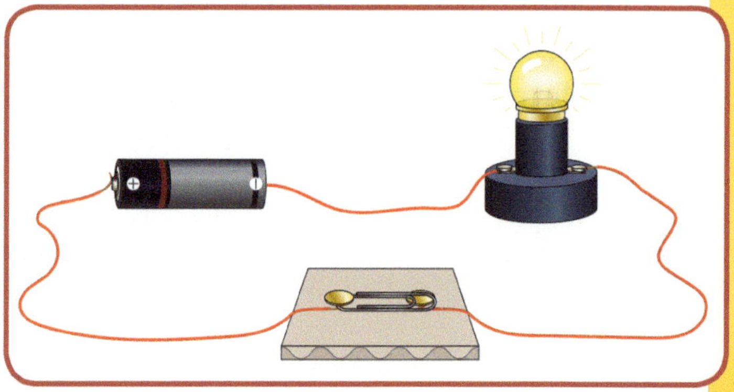

a. Follow the instructions in your Workbook to make a switch like this.

b. Connect the switch in a circuit. What do you observe?

c. Test your switch with different components.

WB 107

4 Switching off some components

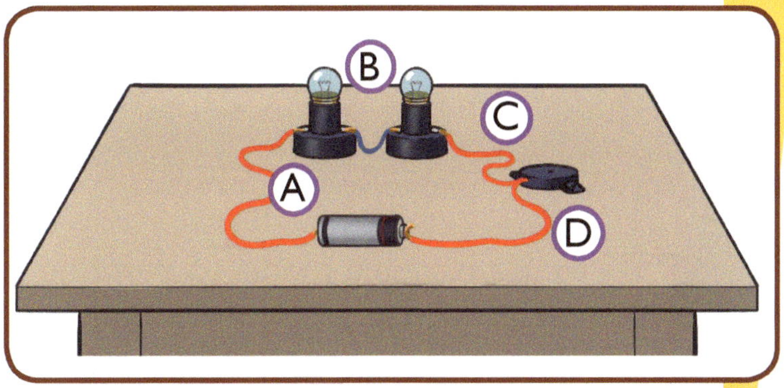

a. Make the circuit shown here.

b. What will happen when you put the switch in the different positions shown? **Plan** how you can find out.

c. Connect the switches as you planned. Present your results.

WB 108

Extension

Try to make switches with some other items your teacher gives you.

a. Which items make the best switch?

b. How can you **design** a switch that you can release quickly using one of these items?

WB 109

Understanding how a switch turns a circuit on or off helps us to design useful applications.

Interesting fact

The switch for the turn signal in a car was invented in the late 1930s. It had two metallic strips that connected and disconnected repeatedly. This completed and broke the circuit, which made the light flash. The same principle is still used today.

Checklist

Complete these statements on page 109 of your Workbook.

- I can describe what happens when there is a break in a circuit.
- I know what the job of a switch is.
- I can explain why a switch is useful in a circuit.
- I can describe how to make a simple switch.

5.3 Models for describing circuits

In this section, I am learning:

- to use a simple model to describe how a circuit works
- about the limits of a model.

Key words

flow
model
particles
represent

What do you think about the children's ideas? Talk about the cartoon with your partner.

Electricity flow

You already know the following about circuits:

- All circuits need a source of energy.
- There must be wires to connect the components to the energy source.
- Components use energy to work.
- The circuit must be complete for the components to work.

We cannot see electricity. But we can explain how it works.

All metals contain millions of tiny electric **particles** called electrons. In a working circuit a force from the battery pushes the particles along through the metal wires. The **flow** of particles is the current. As the particles pass through each component they transfer some of their energy.

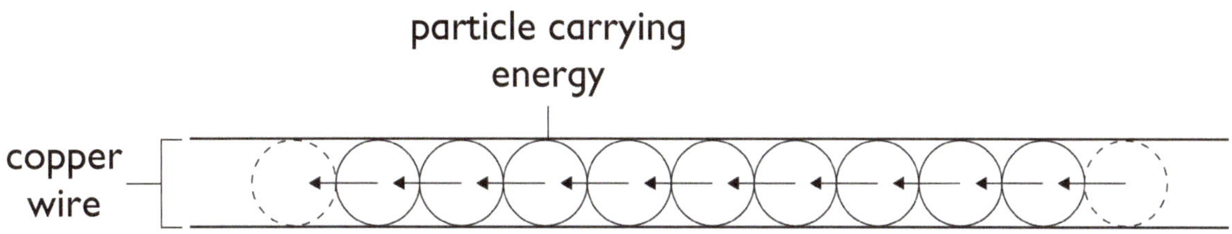

Modelling a circuit

We can use a **model** to help us understand how a circuit works.

1 A human circuit model

Work as a class to make a circuit model, like the one in the picture.

- Your teacher will **represent** the cell.
- Someone will be a circuit component, like a buzzer.
- The rest of you will be the energy particles in the circuit.

What does the model show about how electricity works? Complete the paragraph in your Workbook.

WB 110

There are some differences between the model and a real circuit:

- There are millions of charged particles in a circuit. There were only a few in your circuit.
- The sweets represent small packets of energy. We cannot see or touch energy like we can with sweets.
- The energy source in a real circuit is not a person handing out sweets.

A model helps us to understand something we cannot see or touch.

Extension

A doll's house is a model of a real house.

a. In what ways is it a good model?

b. How is the model not like a real house?

WB 111

2 Adapting a model for different circuits

The model in Activity 1 was for a circuit with one cell and one buzzer. Get into groups and make some changes.

a. How can you change the model to show a circuit with:

- two cells?
- a lamp and a buzzer?
- a switch?

b. Demonstrate your new models to the rest of your class.

WB 111

Interesting fact

The world's largest model railway contains 100 trains that travel along more than 10 km of track. It has more than 3000 miniature buildings in cities and villages.

5.4 Safety with electricity at home

In this section, I am learning:

- that a battery and mains electricity have different voltages
- about the dangers of electricity in the home and how to stay safe.

Key words
danger
mains electricity
safety
voltage

The cell in the photo is labelled 1.5 V. This means 1.5 volts. It is the **voltage** of the cell.

Voltage tells us how much energy the cell can supply. Connecting two 1.5 V cells would make a 3 V battery.

Look at the two lamps in the diagram. One has been connected to a battery that was too strong for the lamp. What has happened?

The electricity in homes and buildings is called **mains electricity**. The electricity comes from a power station. The voltage of mains electricity is 240 V. This is stronger than over a hundred 1.5 V cells. Mains electricity can be very dangerous if we do not use it correctly.

Many appliances in our homes use mains electricity.

Safety with electricity

Electrical circuits can pose **danger**. If we do not work safely with electricity, electrical circuits can be deadly. **Safety** is important.

Most small cells do not transfer much energy. They have a small voltage. Small cells or batteries are usually safe.

But cells do not last forever. A cell contains chemicals to produce energy. If the chemicals leak out, they can be dangerous. This is why you should never put a cell or battery in your mouth.

What does the picture show? Do you think the batteries still work? Talk about your ideas with your partner.

1 Safety at home

Your teacher will show you a video about using electricity safely at home. Write some notes about what you learn in your Workbook.

WB 112

Always use electricity safely to protect yourself.

Do not let an appliance overheat. It can start a fire.

You can experience a big shock if you touch a wire connected to a high voltage. This shock can be deadly.

Never touch a plug with wet hands. You can get shocked.

Always switch off your appliance before touching the plug. Switching off can save your life.

A poster is useful to remind people about working safely with electricity.

2 Making a safety poster

Get into groups. Your teacher will show you some posters.

a. What makes the posters eye-catching?

b. Now design your own poster about safety with electricity for people at home.

c. Share your posters as a class. Do you think the posters are effective?

WB 112–113

Extension

When Nissa uses her hairdryer, she can touch the black cable and not feel any shock. Can you explain why?

WB 113

Interesting fact

Our bodies contain a lot of water. Electricity can flow through water. This means that electricity can travel through us and cause us harm. We could get an electric shock if we touch an open wire.

Checklist

Complete these statements on page 113 of your Workbook.

- I can describe a model that shows how a circuit works.
- I can explain how parts of a model are like the real thing, but others are not.
- I can describe how to change a model to show different circuits.
- I can identify situations where electricity is being used dangerously.
- I can describe how to be safe with electricity.

What have I learnt?

Answer these questions on the worksheet your teacher gives you.

1 Name these components:

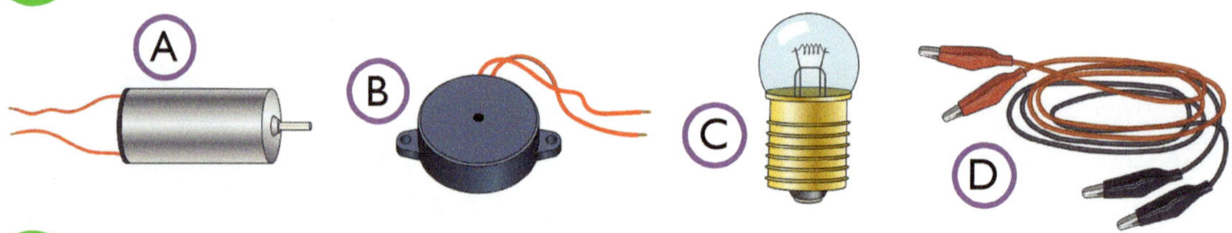

2 Are the statements true or false?

a. All components receive energy from each other.

b. A circuit will work only if there is a break in it.

c. A switch can be either on or off.

3 In which circuit will the lamps be brighter: A or B?

4 Complete these sentences. Choose words from the box.

break component particles cell switch

In a circuit, ____ carry energy from the ____ to a ____. If there is a ____ in the circuit and it is set to the "off" position, a ____ occurs in the circuit and the component does not work.

5 Explain why a switch is useful.

6 Which statement will not help you to work safely with electricity?

a. Always wear gloves when handling a circuit.

b. Never put batteries in your mouth.

c. Keep all liquids away from electricity.

6 Sound

In this unit, I am learning:

- that sounds are made when an object vibrates
- how to measure the loudness of a sound
- that sound travels differently through different materials
- how to block sounds and prevent noise
- about the pitch of a sound.

Key words

decibels
pitch
sound
tuning
vibrate

What sounds might you hear in this scene? How would you describe the sounds? Do you think it would be easy to have a conversation here?

6.1 Exploring how sounds are made

In this section, I am learning:

- that vibrations produce sound
- how different objects produce vibrations
- that sounds can be loud or soft
- how to measure the loudness of sounds.

Key words

decibels
factor
loud
musical instruments
soft
sound
sound level meter
trend
variable
vibrate
voice box
volume

Hearing sounds

We hear **sound** with our ears. People talking, street traffic, music, a telephone ringing and a bird chirping are all examples of sound. They are all different and make us respond in different ways. Our brain helps us to make sense of the sound.

Look at the picture. What sound does an alarm clock make? Do you know how the sound is made? What does the sound tell you?

We can make many different sounds and in many different ways.

1 Making sounds

Your teacher has set up sound stations like this around your classroom.

Get into pairs. Go to three stations.

a. Try to make a sound with the object.

b. What do you see when you make the sound?

c. What is the sound like?

WB 116–117

Extension

Look at the pictures of **musical instruments** in your Workbook.

Which instruments make sound in the same way as the objects at the stations in Activity 1?

WB 117

What causes sound?

In Activity 1 you made sounds by causing something to **vibrate**. When an object vibrates, it moves back and forth very quickly. All sounds come from vibrations.

To make musical sounds, we have to get an instrument to vibrate. When we sing, our vocal cords vibrate.

You can feel the vibrations of your vocal cords when you touch your **voice box**.

2 Good vibrations

Jessica and Simone are both playing an instrument.

Jessica Simone

a. Which instrument do they each play?

b. How does Jessica make her instrument vibrate?

c. How does Simone make her instrument vibrate?

d. Do the instruments sound the same?

WB 118

Loud and soft

The **volume** of a sound describes how **loud** it is. We use a **sound level meter** to measure the loudness of a sound. We measure the loudness of a sound in **decibels** (dB).

3 Measuring sound

Get into groups. Listen to sounds around you.

a. Record their loudness using a sound level meter.

b. What are the loudest and softest sounds?

c. What **trend** do you find?

WB 118–119

How loud are common sounds?

Some sounds around us are loud. Some sounds are **soft**.

The loudness scale below shows the loudness of some common sounds.

Loud sounds close by can damage our ears. Hearing sounds louder than 90 dB for a long time can cause permanent hearing damage.

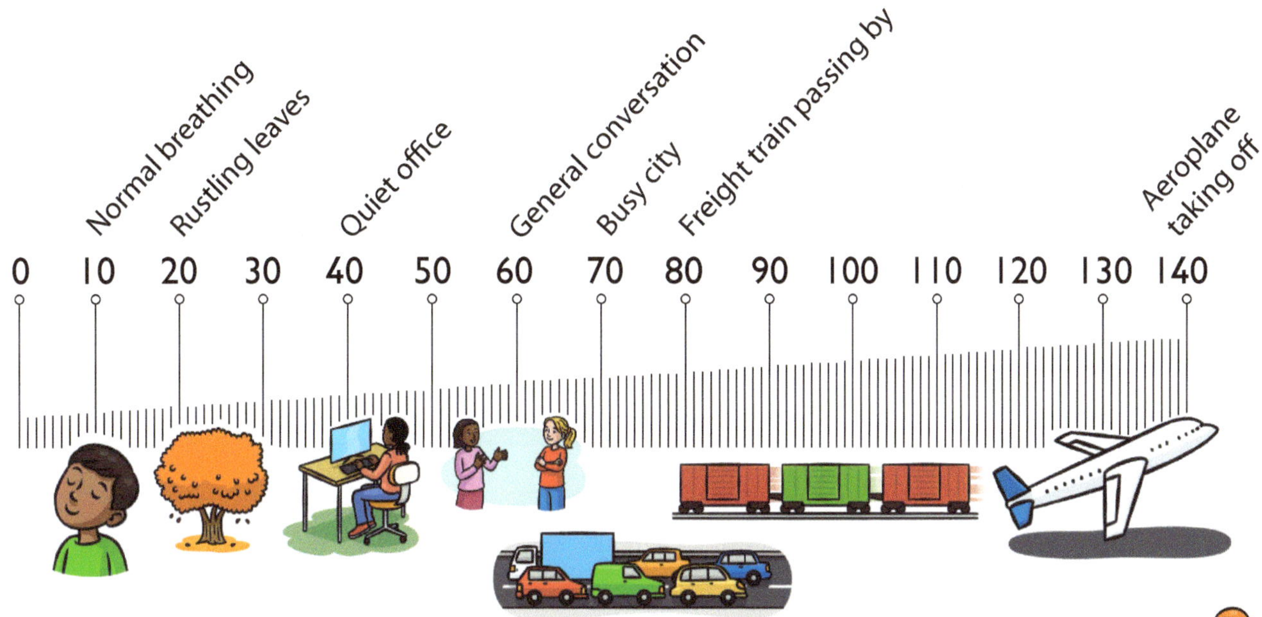

Look at the loudness scale. How loud would whispering in a library be? What about the sound of a lawn mower? Talk about your ideas in your group.

A vibrating object makes the surrounding air vibrate. The vibration energy is passed to other air particles and spreads all around. When the sound reaches your ear it makes your ear vibrate. That's what sound is – vibrations that travel. You can feel these vibrations if you put your hand on a loudspeaker.

4 What happens when you move away from a sound?

Get into groups. Plan an investigation to find out how a sound changes as you move away from it.

a. How will you set up the investigation?

b. What are the variables in your investigation?

c. What result do you predict?

WB 119

Hint

A **variable** is a **factor** you change or control in your investigation.

Extension

Ask your partner to play a musical instrument at different volumes. Do the following each time:

a. Predict the loudness of the sound.

b. Measure the loudness of the sound.

c. See how close your predictions were.

WB 120

Checklist

Complete these statements on page 120 of your Workbook.

- I know that vibrations are the source of sound.
- I can say how different objects, including musical instruments, produce vibrations.
- I can describe how to measure the loudness of a sound.
- I know that loudness is measured in decibels.
- I can investigate how the loudness of a sound changes with distance.

6.2 Sound all around

In this section, I am learning:

- how we hear sounds
- how sound travels through different materials
- why sound travels differently through different materials.

Key words
apparatus
material
sound wave
travel

Sound always starts somewhere. From their source, sounds **travel** through the air to our ears.

Look at the picture. Will Martin's friends all hear the clap at the same time? Will they all hear the sound in the same way? Talk about your ideas in your group.

When vibrations in the air reach our ears, tiny hair cells deep inside our ears pick them up. These cells send a message to the brain, which helps us to understand what the sound was.

You already know that sound travels through air. Air is a gas, which is a type of matter. We can investigate whether sound can also travel through other types of matter.

1 Can sound travel through solids?

Get into pairs. Your teacher will give you some items.

a. Make a simple apparatus as shown in picture A.

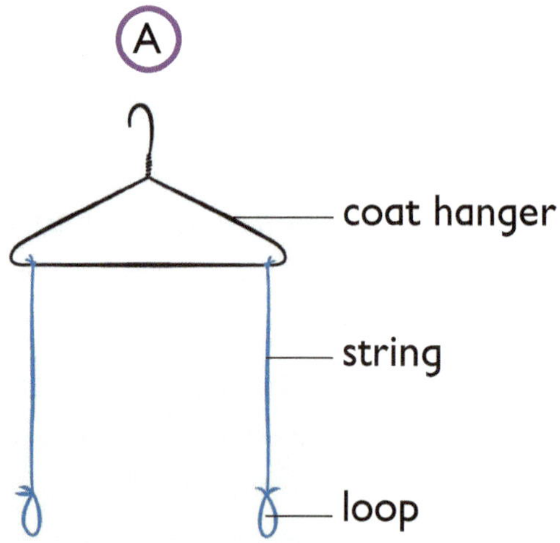

b. Use the apparatus to test whether sound travels through solids. Look at picture B.

c. What do you observe?

WB 121

You now know that sound can travel through a gas and also through solids. Sound can also travel through a liquid.

2 Listening to a sound through a liquid

Get into pairs. Your teacher will give you two metal spoons, a plastic bottle and a bowl of water.

a. Use the bottle to make a simple listening device. Your teacher will show you how.

b. Ask your partner to tap the spoons together in the air. How well can you hear it?

c. Place the listening device in the water. Ask your partner to repeat the sound underwater. How is it different now?

d. What can you conclude?

WB 122

Scientists use devices that work like the one you made in Activity 2 to record sounds underwater. This helps them to understand more about how sea animals communicate.

Dolphins communicate by making sounds and listening to each other underwater.

How sound travels

Sound cannot travel through nothing. Sound needs a **material** to travel through.

A room full of nothing, not even air, would have no sounds at all. In deep space, where there is no air, there is no sound.

Look at the picture. What is the doctor doing? How does the stethoscope help the doctor to hear?

When an object vibrates, the particles of the material around it also vibrate. The particles bump into each other and make more particles vibrate. This transfer of energy is called a **sound wave**. A sound wave keeps going until it runs out of energy.

3 Investigating how sound travels

Someone in your class will go outside and make a loud sound.

How does the sound reach your ears?

Complete the diagram in your Workbook.

WB 123

A telephone allows us to talk to someone out of hearing distance. You can learn about the basic principle of a telephone by making a string telephone.

4 Making a string telephone

Get into pairs.

a. Use the materials your teacher gives you to make a string telephone like in the picture.

b. Test the telephone.

c. Can you explain how the telephone works?

WB 124

Interesting fact

Sound cannot travel in space. An astronaut's helmet has a device that converts sound into a different kind of energy. This energy can travel through space and is then converted back into sound so a listener can hear what an astronaut says.

6.3 How to block sounds

In this section, I am learning:

- about different materials that can prevent sound from reaching our ears
- why blocking sound from our ears is important
- how we can avoid hearing noise.

Key words
noise
prevent

Sometimes we want to **prevent** sound from travelling to our ears. Loud sounds can damage our ears. Wearing ear defenders when working with noisy machines helps to protect our ears.

Look at the picture. How do you think ear defenders protect our ears? Where else have you seen people wearing ear defenders?

The material a sound travels through affects the quality of the sound. Some solids are better at letting sound through than others.

1 Measuring the loudness of a sound through different solids

Work as a class.

a. Plan an investigation to find out how well sound travels through different solids.

b. Then perform the investigation. How does the evidence link to what you know about vibrations? Complete the paragraph in your Workbook.

Hint

Remember to think about how to set up a fair test and how you will present your results.

WB 125–126

Noise

Unwanted sounds are called **noise**. What is noise to one person may be music to someone else. We can use our knowledge of how sound travels to reduce the noise we hear around us.

What plan has Josh made to avoid listening to noise? Does Annabelle think her violin makes a noise? Share your ideas with your teacher.

Musicians often use soundproof rooms to practise or record music. Sound cannot escape from the room. Materials that are good at blocking sound are fitted to the walls of a soundproof room.

Practising music in a soundproof room means other people will not be disturbed.

2 Investigating how to block sound

Get into groups. Imagine you have been asked to design a soundproof music room.

Your teacher will give you some materials.

a. Plan how to investigate which material will be best for a soundproof room. Describe your planned investigation in your Workbook.

b. Explain the reasons for your material choices.

WB 126–127

✓ Checklist

Complete these statements on page 127 of your Workbook.

- I know that sound travels from its source to our ears.
- I know that sound needs a material to travel through.
- I can compare how sound travels through solids, liquids and gases.
- I can explain why sound travels better through some materials than others.
- I discovered that some materials are better than others at blocking sound.

6.4 Investigating pitch

Key words
brass
high
low
pattern
percussion
pitch
string
tuning
tuning fork
woodwind

In this section, I am learning:

- about the sound of different instruments
- about the pitch of a sound
- how the pitch of a sound can change
- how to make high and low sounds, and loud and soft sounds, with musical instruments.

Which instruments do you see in the picture? Do they all sound the same?

In an orchestra many different instruments play together. They produce vibrations in different ways.

- Violins and cellos are **string** instruments. They produce vibrations when the strings are stroked or plucked.
- **Brass** and **woodwind** instruments, such as a trumpet or a flute, have a long tube in which air vibrates.
- A **percussion** instrument, such as a drum, makes a sound when it is struck.

The pitch of a sound

The speed of the vibrations makes the sounds **high** or **low**. These words describe the **pitch** of a sound.

A note with a high pitch sound is caused by fast vibrations.

A note with a low pitch sound is caused by slow vibrations.

1 Different instruments, different sounds

Select one of the instruments in the pictures. Describe to your partner the different sounds that can come from the instrument.

WB 128

A thin or short string, a short tube and a small drum can be used to make high sounds.

If you want to make a low sound, you should use a longer and thicker string, a longer tube or a wider drum.

2 Can you tell a high pitch from a low pitch?

Get into pairs. Listen to the sounds your teacher plays.

Which are high? Which are low?

WB 128

Put your fingers on your voice box. Sing a high note. Then sing a low note. What do you notice about where the sound comes from?

High notes and low notes have a different pitch, but they can be equally loud or equally soft.

Extension

You now have four words to describe sounds:

- "high" and "low" for pitch
- "loud" and "soft" for volume.

Which combination of words describe these sounds best?

- The crash of cymbals
- The sound of thunder
- A whisper to a friend
- Your heartbeat
- Distant birdsong

WB 129

Making music with glasses of water

We can use a glass to create vibrations that make sound. We can do this by tapping a glass gently with the handle of a wooden spoon, carefully rubbing the rim with a finger, or blowing across a bottle opening.

We can use glasses with different amounts of water to create different pitches.

When we play music, we put notes of different pitches together in a **pattern**. **Tuning** an instrument to a specific pitch lets us create music that is easy to listen to. We use a **tuning fork** to tune an instrument.

3 Making your own music

Get into groups to form a band with glass instruments.

a. Experiment with the sound of your instrument.

b. Put the sounds together in a short pattern and make some music.

WB 129

4 Investigating sounds with different liquids

Get into your glass band again. This time use some cooking oil rather than water for your instruments.

a. Try to recreate the pitches you used in Activity 3.

b. Write your observations in your Workbook.

WB 130

Interesting fact

Bats can hear sounds with a much higher pitch than humans can. Elephants can hear sounds with a much lower pitch than humans can.

Checklist

Complete these statements on page 130 of your Workbook.

- I can identify the sounds of different instruments.
- I know that "high" and "low" describe the pitch of a sound.
- I can recognise different pitches.
- I can make high, low, loud and soft sounds.

What have I learnt?

Answer these questions on the worksheet your teacher gives you.

1 Put these activities in order from loudest to softest.

Noisy restaurant	Rock concert	People in a library

2 Which statement is false?

a. Sounds are caused by vibrations.

b. A high sound is made by slow vibrations.

c. Sound can pass through a solid.

3 What are the units for measuring the loudness of sound?

4 Janice hears her sister playing the guitar in the next room. Arrange these sentences in order to tell the story of how the sound gets to Janice.

a. The sound energy travelled through the solid wall.

b. The sound moved through the air in Janice's bedroom to her ears.

c. The string made the air vibrate.

d. Sound travelled from the guitar through the air in the next room.

e. First the guitar string was plucked.

5 Which two objects can be used to make a string telephone?

plastic cup	bathroom towel	
glass of water	ball of string	football

6 Name one instrument that often makes very high sounds and one that makes very low sounds.

Glossary

animals	Living creatures that breathe, grow and move around on their own.
ankle	The joint between the lower leg and the foot, which allows the foot to move.
apparatus	Materials or equipment used to carry out investigations or experiments.
arms	Limbs of the upper body, which connect the hands and wrists to the shoulders.
attract	To pull an object towards another without touching.
bar chart	A graph that consists of horizontal or vertical bars to show the pattern of results.
bar magnet	A magnet in the shape of a bar with its magnetic poles at either end.
battery	A group of cells, all connected, which serves as the source of energy in an electrical circuit.
boil	To let a liquid heat up to the point where it starts to bubble; water boils at 100 °C.
bone	The hard material that makes up the skeleton of a vertebrate's body.
brass	A class of musical instruments made of a yellow metal (brass).
break	To end or interrupt the flow of electricity in an electrical circuit.
brick wall	A wall made out of hard blocks of baked clay.
bubbles	Small pockets of gas surrounded by a liquid.
buzzer	An electrical device that makes a sound when electricity passes through it.
cell	A single component that provides energy in an electrical circuit; two or more cells connected together make up a battery.
circuit	A complete path around which electricity flows.
collect	To gather together or capture.
compare	To look at the similarities and differences between two or more things.
compass	An instrument with a small magnetic needle, which points north.
complete (circuit)	Without breaks or gaps.
component	A part of something.
conclusion	A decision made after carefully studying the results of an experiment.
condense	To let a gas change to a liquid.
connector	A device that joins two objects together.

construct	To build or put something together.
contract	To become shorter or tighter (when speaking about muscles).
cool	To lose heat.
copper	A reddish-brown non-magnetic metal. Copper is often used to make pipes, as it does not easily rust, or wires, as it is a good conductor of electricity.
creatures	Another word for animals, big or small.
crocodile clip	A sprung metal clip with jagged edges used to connect components in an electrical circuit.
cure	To make a sick person better or healthy.
current	The flow of charged particles in an electrical circuit.
danger	The possibility of something bad or harmful happening.
decibels	The unit for measuring the loudness of sound.
design	To make detailed plans for something.
developments	Human (construction) activities that change the environment or local area.
disasters	Events that cause lots of damage to the environment or human communities.
discuss	To talk to other people about something.
drip	To flow downwards in small drops.
earthquakes	Events during which the ground shakes heavily; may cause the ground to split and buildings to fall.
elbow	The joint between the upper and lower arm, which allows the arm to bend.
electricity	A form of energy used to make circuits work.
environment	The space and conditions around living things.
equipment	The materials, apparatus or tools used for a particular activity.
evaporation	The process when a liquid changes to a gas.
evidence	The available information for proving that something is true.
explain	To make or give reasons for.
factor	Something that has an influence on a situation or causes something to happen.
fair test	An investigation to compare two of the same things treated differently in only one way; all the other things in the test stays the same.
features	The characteristics or properties of something.
feet	The body parts at the end of the legs, used to stand on and to walk.
fingers	The body parts at the end of each hand.
floating magnet	Two magnets above and below each other that are held together without touching each other by a magnetic force.
flow	To move in a smooth, steady stream without interruption.

force	A push or a pull on an object to make it move, slow down, change direction or change shape.
fracture	A broken bone.
freeze, freezing	To cool a liquid enough to turn it into a solid; water freezes at 0 °C.
gas	A substance in which the particles are far apart and spread out to fill the available space; air is a gas.
gold	A soft, heavy, yellow metal that can be easily shaped and is non-magnetic. Gold is valuable and is often used to make jewellery.
habitat	The place where an animal or a plant lives.
heat	To add energy to a substance, causing its temperature to rise.
high	Describes a sound with a raised pitch.
hip	The joint that connects the top of the thigh to the rest of the body.
horseshoe magnet	A magnet in the shape of a horseshoe with its magnetic poles at either end.
human	A person.
identification key	A set of questions about an organism's features used to identify it.
identify	To recognise or be able to name someone or something.
invertebrates	Animals that do not have a backbone or hard skeleton inside their bodies.
iron	A strong, heavy, grey metal that is magnetic and easily rusts.
keepers	Iron or steel bars placed across the poles of a magnet to protect the magnetic strength of the magnet.
knee	The joint between the upper and lower leg, which allows the leg to bend.
lamp	A circuit component that gives off light when electricity runs through it.
lamp holder	A box or compartment for holding a lamp or bulb to keep it in position in a circuit.
leaf pile	A pile of leaves that acts as a habitat for small animals.
liquid	A substance in which the particles are fairly far apart but still touching one another; it flows and can be poured; oil is a liquid.
litter	Rubbish such as paper, cans or bottles thrown on the ground.
local	Describes an area or conditions near an organism.
log pile	A pile of logs that acts as a habitat for small animals.
loud	Describes a sound that can easily be heard.
low	Describes a sound that is reduced in pitch.
magnet	A metal object that attracts magnetic materials and other magnets.
magnetic	Able to be attracted to a magnet.
mains electricity	The electricity supplied by power stations and used in buildings for lighting, heating and making machines work.
materials	Substances that objects are made from.

matter	The scientific word for what everything is made from; matter exists in three states, namely solids, liquids or gases.
meadow	An open field of grass, growing wild or used to grow hay.
measure	To find the exact size, weight or amount of something using a ruler, scale or other measuring device.
measurements	The exact size or dimensions of something that is found by measuring.
medicine	Tablets or liquids given to people to cure illnesses or make them feel better.
melt, melting	To heat a solid so that it turns into a liquid.
metal	A solid, shiny material that can conduct heat and electricity; some metals are also magnetic.
model	Something used to show how something else looks or works.
motor	A circuit component that changes electrical energy into movement energy.
move	To go from one place to another.
muscles	Long elastic fibres (tissues) attached to the bones in the body of a human or animal, which allow the bones to move.
musical instruments	Objects that make musical sounds.
natural disasters	Natural events that cause large-scale damage to the environment or communities.
neck	The part of the body that joins the head to the shoulders.
noise	Unwanted sounds.
north	Identifies one pole of a magnet.
observe	To notice something.
oil slick	A thick layer of oil floating on water.
particles	The tiny parts that make up all matter.
pattern	The specific arrangement of shapes or items that can be repeated.
percussion	Describes a class of instruments that produce sound when hit, such as drums and cymbals.
pitch	A measure of how high or low a sound is.
plan	To put together a detailed list of steps for doing a task.
plants	Living things that make their own food using air, water and sunlight.
poles	The two opposite ends of a magnet.
pollution	Anything that spoils the environment.
pond	An area of still water that acts as a habitat for water plants or animals.
pooter	An apparatus used to collect small invertebrates, such as insects.
pour	To let a substance flow in a steady stream.
powder	A mass of dry dust or very small pieces of a material made by crushing or grinding a solid.

predict	To suggest what might happen in future based on what you already know.
prevent	To stop something from happening.
record	To write down or display findings.
recycle	To collect waste materials and make them into new materials so they can be reused.
relax	To return back to its original state or length; the opposite of contract.
reliable	Able to be trusted.
repeat	To do something again in the same way.
repel	To push something away without touching.
represent	To be an example of something.
results	Findings or information discovered through experimentation or investigation.
reversible	Able to be turned back to the original state.
ribs	The bones that form a cage around the chest of a human or animal.
safety	The state of being safe or free from harm.
select	To choose something from a list or group.
shin	The front part of the leg between the knee and the ankle.
shoulders	The part of the body between the neck and upper arm.
silver	A soft, shiny, white metal that can be easily shaped. Often used to make jewellery. Also a word used to describe a light-grey colour.
skeleton	An inner frame made of bone that supports an animal's body and protects its organs.
skull	The bony case that forms the head of an animal's body and protects the brain.
soft	Describes a quiet sound.
solid	A material in which the particles have a fixed, regular arrangement; a solid is usually hard and has a fixed shape.
sound	Anything that people or animals can hear with their ears.
sound level meter	A device used to measure the loudness of a sound.
sound wave	The pattern in which sound energy travels through a material.
south	Identifies the pole of a magnet opposite to north.
spine	The string of bones running along the back of a human or vertebrate animal.
steel	A hard, strong metal made from iron that is magnetic. Often used for making machines, cars and tools.
stones	Small pieces of rock.
string	A class of instruments that produce sound when a thin, tight cord or thread vibrates.
suggest	To put forward an idea.

switch	A circuit component that can break or complete a circuit.
symptoms	Signs shown by the body when it is unwell or has an illness.
table	A set of rows and columns for displaying findings or information.
temperature	A measurement of how hot or cold something is.
test	To try something to find out information.
thermometer	A device used for measuring temperature.
thigh	Part of the leg between the hip and the knee.
thumbs	The short, thick first fingers on the hands of humans and primates.
travel	To move from one place to another.
trend	A pattern of results.
tsunami	A very large destructive sea wave caused by an earthquake or volcanic eruption.
tuning	Adjusting a musical instrument so that it plays notes at the correct pitch.
tuning fork	A tool used to tune a musical instrument.
variables	The factors in an investigation.
vertebrae	The many short bones that make up the spine.
vertebrate	An animal that has a backbone and bones inside its body.
vibrate	To move forwards and backwards between two points very quickly.
voice box	The structure at the top of the windpipe that contains the vocal chords, which produce sound when we speak or sing.
volcano	A mountain with an opening at the top through which lava, ash and gases escape from inside the Earth.
voltage	The strength of electricity.
volume	The loudness of a sound.
wand magnet	A magnet in the shape of a wand with its magnetic poles at either end.
water vapour	Water as a gas.
wire	A strand of metal used in an electrical circuit.
working circuit	A complete electrical circuit that functions (works) correctly with no breaks (gaps) in the circuit.
woodland	An area of land covered in trees or forest.
woodwind	A group of musical instruments that were originally made of wooden tubes.
wrist	The joint between the hand and the arm, which allows the hand to move.
X-ray	An invisible ray of light used to take photographs of the bones inside the body.